PERSPECTIVES ON ORGANIZATIONS:

Schools in the Larger Social Environment

by

Ronald G. Corwin and Roy A. Edelfelt

Edited by

Theodore E. Andrews and Brenda L. Bryant

American Association of Colleges
for Teacher Education
and
Association of Teacher Educators
Washington, D.C.

CONTENTS

Introduction *Inside Front Cover*
Editors and Contributors *Inside Back Cover*
Foreword *iii*
Preface *iv*
Volume Overview *1*

PART I. READINGS ON THE SOCIAL
ENVIRONMENT OF SCHOOLS
   The Limits of Local Control Over Education *3*
   School Governance and Its Community Sociopolitical
     Environment *37*
     Laurence Iannaccone
   Government's Responsibility in Improving
     Education Outcomes *56*
     William L. Smith

PART II. SCHOOLS, COMMUNITIES, AND TEACHERS
IN ACTION
   Activity 1. The Choate County Textbook Controversy:
     Cultures in Clash *67*
   Activity 2. *Conrack* *85*
   Activity 3. Alternate Concepts of Power and Leadership *90*
     Frankie Beth Nelson
   Activity 4. Ethnomethodology *95*
     Laurel Richardson Walum

POSTSCRIPT *114*

APPENDIX *119*

Foreword

This volume is the third in a series which the American Association of Colleges for Teacher Education (AACTE) and the Association of Teacher Education (ATE) have jointly published in collaboration with the Teacher Corps. It represents an effort by nationally renowned authors who have studied the dynamics of schools as organizations. As schools and communities have become more complex and as society has required schools to take on more and diversified tasks, the need for pre- and inservice education personnel to understand the dynamics of their teaching context has increased. At one time someone facetiously commented that curriculum is what happens when a teacher closes the door and starts to teach. There can be no self-contained classroom nor self-sufficient school today. Education personnel are part of a social system that exists within a school building and system as well as in the larger community and society.

As organizations committed to the improvement of teacher education, we have joined in this venture to increase the professional knowledge base on a most important topic. We encourage our colleagues to read the two earlier volumes in the series: *Perspectives on Organizations: Viewpoints for Teachers,* Vol. I (Washington, D.C.: AACTE & ATE, 1976, 86 pp.) and *Perspectives on Organizations: The School as a Social Organization,* Vol. II (Washington, D.C.: AACTE & ATE, 1977, 113 pp.). We recommend that professors and school inservice coordinators review the three-part series as possible basic resource materials for formal and informal studies. We ask that responsible education leaders encourage libraries in colleges, in school districts, and in state education agencies to include the series in their collections. We encourage state units of our organizations to study the series for possible use in their state meetings.

In publishing this three-part series, AACTE and ATE do not necessarily endorse the interpretation and recommendation stated implicitly or explicitly. We are publishing the series as part of our continuing efforts to promote study, discussion, and action to improve teacher education. We believe that this series can be a good stimulus to such actions.

We commend a number of people who, in cooperation with the writers and the substantive editors listed on the title page, have made this volume possible.

We acknowledge with appreciation the encouragement of and funding by the Teacher Corps which have made the series possible.

J. T. Sandefur, President
American Association of Colleges
for Teacher Education

Marvin Henry, President
Association of Teacher Educators

June 1978

Preface

The Teacher Corps conducted its first national training institute in the summer of 1975. New project interns and team leaders, called corpsmembers, were participants in four intense weeks at the University of Richmond. In scope and content the institute was a unique response. Needs gave it birth; and evaluation studies, project directors, and research on the management of change gave it focus. The experience, known as the Corps Members Training Institute (CMTI), was repeated for other corpsmembers in 1976 at Florida State University in Tallahassee, and in 1977 at San Diego State University.

The major impetus for the whole idea must be credited to third-party program evaluations. More than one of these pointed up the great need for interns to understand the organizational features of schools. The Corwin Study in 1973 particularly described how crucial it was for our teaching teams, and particularly the interns, to understand the implications of organizational characteristics and realize that schools are social systems. The Marsh Study in 1974 reinforced this point.

Additionally, project directors were reporting that Teacher Corps interns needed an esprit de corps, a personal identification with the national program effort. It also seemed to directors that a common training session could be the most realistic and profound cross-cultural learning and living experience ever provided by the Teacher Corps.

Finally, the research literature on the management of change and theories on the processes of change have important implications for teacher education. The Teacher Corps program is designed to help schools and colleges effect change. In the early history of the Corps, a basic assumption existed that interns, acting as change agents, could reform the school merely with their commitment and presence. This proved to be an unrealistic and unproductive assumption. We have now been careful to insist that Teacher Corps interns are not, and should not attempt to be, change agents. Our expectation is simply that they will be the best and most highly qualified teachers available to the profession, not in the traditional sense as dispensers of knowledge, but as facilitators of the learning process. This new role requires more and different theory and training than has been the case typically in teacher education. It starts with the assumption that facilitating means managing. Teachers must manage processes, products, and young people in an organized manner if they want and expect positive growth and change to occur in the learning and behavior of their students. This seems most accomplishable when the school is viewed as a formal organization, as a social system, and the classrooms in that school as subsystems. This systemic approach treats the classroom as an organization within an organization—the school.

Previous teacher training programs, which focused on the individual teacher learner, tended to provide new knowledge or skills to that teacher learner but did not have impact for change on the school to which the teacher returned. In many cases the teacher's new knowledge became a threat to teaching peers who had not themselves benefited from such training. Administrators were often threatened when the teacher attempted to implement this knowledge and skill. We now know how these problems can be avoided. Many of us have come to believe that for the institutionalized growth and development of educational personnel, and for impact on the school, the school as an organization is the smallest unit of change. Similarly, for the institutionalized growth and development of children, the classroom is the smallest unit of change.

Systems theory and organizational behavior theory have an important place in the conceptualization of preservice and inservice education. Many good and talented teachers feel unable to use their talents effectively because they believe the hierarchical structure of administrators, supervisors, and the environmental field force known as "the community" have placed unwarranted constraints upon them. This sense of alienation and powerlessness in the finest teachers will obviously prove contagious. Idealistic beginners will, therefore, hardly be immune. Teacher Corps is persuaded that if schools, as social systems, are to be changed for the better, everyone with a role or investment in the education and/or schooling of children must be collaboratively involved in the change process. If both new and experienced teachers were to have an opportunity to study the nature of organizations and the ways members interact, they might find that certain behavior characteristics manifested in schools are found in most organizations. Even more important, these behaviors can be understood and dealt with.

We know, of course, that most of the scientific data on organization are found in studies of economic and industrial organizations. Over the past few years, universities have conducted numerous educational organization studies in educational administration for middle managers and school superintendents, initially supported through the Kellogg Foundation Program. No one, it seemed, had begun to develop concepts, theoretical formulations, and case studies for prospective and practicing teachers to use in studying the school as a formal organization. With the exception of the initial work on organization study done by Chris Argyris for employees, little else had been developed for a role group below that of administrators and managers. Someone somewhere had to begin.

The Corps Member Training Institutes were seen as having three goals. The first was to develop an esprit de corps among our newest members. The second was to provide them with a rich multicultural experience. The third was to involve them and their experienced teacher team leader in an academic experience designed to open their eyes to theories of organization, both structure and behavior, and to the many styles of learning and teaching there are. The first Institute was organized into the two separate graduate-level strands, Organization Perspectives, and Teaching and Learning Style Analysis. This volume is the third of a series of three dealing with Perspectives on Organizations. We hope to use this series as part of the curriculum of future CMTI's.

The Teacher Corps is pleased to have the American Association of Colleges for Teacher Education and the Association of Teacher Educators serve as joint publishers of this volume. Their constituencies are important ones in any effort to implement change in the preparation of education personnel. Their effort is to provide practitioners, decision-makers, and researchers with the ideas and information which can become building steps to progress.

This volume, like the preceding ones, offers those who may share our concerns about some of the papers, other materials and procedures that were used to give corpsmembers and team leaders a new perspective on organizations particularly, as the subtitle states, on the social environment of schools.

The contents of this volume were selected from materials prepared for CMTI, 1975. Jim Steffensen and Beryl Nelson of my staff are to be commended for having worked so closely with the publication's editors on each of these volumes.

These represent beginnings, at least, of a response to a serious need. Each of the three volumes reinforces the fact that the study of organizations is no luxury item in a realistic program of teacher training.

William L. Smith
Director
Teacher Corps

June 1978

Volume Overview*

Part I of this volume is titled *Readings on the Social Environment of Schools*. The purpose of the readings is to examine some environmental factors, external to the school, that impact directly on school policies and practices. In "The Limits of Local Control Over Education, Sections I,II," Ronald Corwin and Roy Edelfelt discuss citizen participation in the schools. Laurence Iannaccone is concerned about the politics of American education, and about the relationship between the schools and the state in particular, in "School Governance and its Sociopolitical Environment." "Government's Responsibility in Improving Education Outcomes" is the title and the theme of the reading by William Smith. He directs his attention to the federal role in education.

Part II provides an opportunity for readers and instructors to explore many of the issues raised in Part I. *Schools, Communities, and Teachers in Action* is a series of activities designed to be used in an instructional setting. They may be used in any order. Each activity stresses the complex interrelationships among schools and their local, state, or federal sociopolitical environments. Included in this section are:

- A case study, "The Choate County Textbook Controversy: Cultures in Clash;"
- A film, *"Conrack;"*
- A reading for discussion, "Alternate Concepts of Power and Leadership;" and
- A series of structured exercises to explore some assumptions about behavior or "Ethnomethodology."

After an initial reading of Part I, readers should select an activity in Part II to explore concepts in more depth. Readers will want to continue to relate Parts I and II to each other. Instructors will find the "Instructional Mode, Goals, and Objectives," reprinted from Volume I and contained in the Appendix, of value in planning for student sessions.

Ronald G. Corwin, Columbus, Ohio
Roy A. Edelfelt, Washington, D.C.

June 1978

---

*Sections that do not have specific author cited were written by Ronald G. Corwin and Roy A. Edelfelt.

Part I
Readings on the Social Environment of Schools

The Limits of Local Control Over Education, Section I: Citizen Participation at the Local Level

Ronald G. Corwin   Roy A. Edelfelt

The growth of bureaucracy and professionalism in modern society seems to have reduced the opportunities for individual citizens to participate in and to influence matters of vital concern to them and their children. These circumstances have raised several types of concerns, including: a conflict between bureaucracy and democracy; the inability of citizens to control nearly autonomous public organizations; and the tendency for organizations to lose sight of the goals which they were intended to achieve.

BUREAUCRACY VERSUS DEMOCRACY

Since Weber first warned of totalitarian tendencies within large-scale organizations, social scientists, policy makers and other informed citizens have pondered the threat that bureaucracy poses to democracy. Service organizations are like other organizations in the fact that they are often controlled by a few persons. School systems are not immune from oligarchical control. Moreover, within school organizations, the top echelon is often the captive of powerful political elites, while the lower echelons often appear to be closed to influence from individuals outside the organization. Employees of such organizations do not have to be responsive to outsiders' desires and criticisms. Indeed, some writers believe it is unrealistic to expect that employees working within bureaucratized service organizations will be responsive to the various desires of their clients or even treat their clients humanely.

The problem is especially pronounced in schools serving low-income neighborhoods. Although the middle-income groups are not entirely effective in working with bureaucracies, they do have certain advantages over their low-income counterparts. They are probably a little more accustomed to working in bureaucracies, and are relatively more experienced in coping with them. Moreover, bureaucratic systems largely reflect the interest of the dominant social class. Indeed, some critics argue that bureaucratic organizations tend to penalize those employees who identify too closely with their low-income clients. These critics maintain that professional organizations are least able to serve precisely the neighborhoods with the most severe personal and social problems, i.e., those with high unemployment rates, language differences, high turnover of residents, and high rates of disease, mental illness, homicide, crime, and juvenile delinquency. There are several reasons behind these charges. Service organizations are governed by general rules which do not always fit the special circumstances of low-income neighborhoods, and therefore employees will encounter difficulties within the organization as they try to meet the needs of those they are trying to help. These agencies are expected to assist as many people as possible, and it is easier to meet the quotas by concentrating on the simpler, less time-consuming cases that are more typical of the middle-class clients. Also, the fact that different service agencies specialize in specific problems makes it difficult for the clients who are afflicted with many problems to find meaningful coordinated assistance.

Low-income groups have become more vocal about some of these problems, and many people have become more socially conscious about the injustices that some individuals have experienced in their encounters with service organizations. While citizen participation is often proposed as a panacea, it is not always the answer. Selznick (1949) undertook a study to determine whether it is possible for citizens to participate effectively in an agency of the federal government operating at the grass roots level of local communities, and his conclusion is a sobering one. He found that local citizens used the programs to satisfy their own private interests, which were at variance with the larger society's interests—the very ones that prompt national social programs in the first place. In this case at least, citizen control diverted the program from its original goals, thus defeating some of the explicit purposes it was designed to fulfill. The study then, raised questions about how to achieve *balanced* participation which would not jeopardize the general welfare.

ORGANIZATIONAL AUTONOMY AND DEPENDENCE

A related concern is the fact that in a public organization, lay persons outside of it are legally in charge, and yet the organization must have a certain amount of latitude or autonomy from such outside control in order for its members to act rationally and maintain standards essential for effective performance. All organizations seek to gain power over those on whom they depend. In Thomson's (1967, p. 3) words:

> The public school, for example, which is constrained to accept virtually all students of a specified age, under conditions of population growth has urgent need

for power with respect to those in the environment who control financial and other inputs. If the environment imposes mandatory loads, the school must seek power with respect to resources.

He observes that since the public holds organizations responsible for their actions, organizations try to control their circumstances by sealing off important aspects of their work from outside influence as a means of maintaining control over their own processes and goals. For the same reason, professional employees often try to expand their influence over all aspects of their clients' lives as a means of increasing control over their circumstances.

Professionals are licensed on the assumption that they will use their power to protect clients from the arbitrary aspects of overpowering bureaucracies. Sometimes they do. But it doesn't always work that way. Instead, professionalism can create other problems over and above those which stem from the bureaucratic system. Freidson (1970) maintains that the expertise of professionals in our society has been institutionalized into something similar to a bureaucratic office. Their favored positions give professionals an inordinate degree of autonomy that enables them to remain insensitive to the welfare of their clients. Unlike bureaucrats, professionals are imputed with unquestioned objectivity based on their expertise and on scientific truth. This image helps to immunize them from higher review and outside scrutiny. Freidson charges that professions are often primarily interested in advancing policies that will enhance their control. For example, professionals gain the right to withhold information on the assumption that the client is incapable of understanding or would act irresponsibly with the knowledge imparted.

These general observations help to explain some problems associated with the governance of education today. If schools are to maintain their objectivity, to uphold standards of fairness, and to enforce academic standards, they must be given some independence from parents and other citizens. This does not mean that they can ever be entirely independent, because they depend upon taxpayers, employers, and other outsiders for support and resources. They need the backing of parents to encourage children to do their homework assignments and to reinforce the discipline imposed by teachers. They also expect outsiders to employ and utilize their products. But as teachers have professionalized and claimed the perogatives of other professions there have been growing concerns that other checks are needed.

In education it is important to distinguish between organizational autonomy and professional autonomy. The school as an organization has justified its autonomy on the basis of a broad societal commitment to educating the young, and the necessity of remaining free from provincialism and the vested interests of particular clients. Its professional staff is presumed to have competence and enlightened purpose, which should not be disturbed by special interests or narrow thinking. Ensurances have been granted for academic freedom, tenure, and due process for professionals charged with malpractice or unethical conduct.

However, the case for the autonomy of teaching as a profession, in other words, insisting that educators have complete control of professional circumstances, has not been as convincing. The public is not confident about teachers' expertise, and the scientific basis of classroom teaching has not been well established. Also, teaching is clearly a public profession. Elementary and secondary schools have almost always been under public control in the United States. Typically, educators have not insisted on controlling schools, because control is established by law as a public, state responsibility. They have, on the other hand, attempted to gain control of the teaching profession in regard to both preparation and practice, and while their right to control is still controversial even among educators, it is nevertheless beginning to be achieved in a few states. It is, however, a significant demand which indirectly could lead to greater control of schools as well.

The implications are enormous. Professional people often have a difficult time collaborating meaningfully with lay persons who do not understand the intricacies of the profession. The problems of working with clients with social backgrounds different from those of the professionals are especially acute. The fact that most professions are poorly integrated into the lives or the communities of low-income clients can hamper the ability to serve the poor. A special problem for professionals in dealing with low-income clients is that social class and educational level are in large degree coterminous. Young people from low-income families who become teachers join the middle class by virtue of their college education. Their upward social mobility is often characterized by the "conversion syndrome," that is the tendency of people with a newly achieved social status to ardently defend the norms of the group they have just joined, and, conversely, their self-conscious effort to reject the norms associated with their prior circumstances. Human services professions, particularly teaching, have always attempted to impose middle-class moral standards as a condition for providing low-income clients with a professional service, and this attitude creates almost insurmountable chasms of social distance from these clients. It is possible for teachers to collaborate with parents in low-income neighborhoods only to the extent that there is mutual respect. Unfortunately, respect for the dignity of all human beings has yet to be made a dictum of professional practice.

A profession, says Etzioni (1964), is a special case of separating "consumption" from "control." This separation typically occurs with the process of bureaucratization. He believes that consumers must somehow regain at least some control. Of course, few educators or clients seek complete or unilateral control. Rather, it is a question of establishing zones of autonomy for both educators and citizens. The challenge is to find an appropriate balance so that school programs clearly represent what clients want, yet allow sufficient autonomy for professionals to practice as their expertise and ethics dictate. In the final analysis, there are two ways of breaking up a professional group's monopoly to protect the client from exploitation: by establishing communication bridges and by building bases of countervailing consumer power. To the extent that educators do not take the initiative in establishing the first alternative, citizens will find it necessary to undertake the second.

GOAL DISPLACEMENT

Similar themes punctuate the literature on organizational administration concerned with the inflexibility of organizations and their unresponsiveness to change. Organizations rely upon uniform policies to achieve coordination. These policies are expressed in rules, procedures, narrow specialization, and red tape. Employees who are charged with upholding this system sometimes manifest a "bureaucratic personality." That is, they become inflexible and indifferent to the needs of individual citizens by virtue of the fact that they have a disproportionate amount of power to interpret and enforce the rules, and tend to view clients only from the standpoint of their narrow specialization. They are naturally preoccupied with predictable and short-run problems, and in the process can easily forget clients' desires and the ultimate goals of the organization. If rules are rigid, and the monitoring of their behavior is strict, employees can become so preoccupied with satisfying the requirements of the organizational system and with coping and survival, that they become reluctant to use their initiative and imagination in the interests of the clients whom they serve.

However, it is by no means clear that bureaucracies *always* induce so much defensiveness in employees. Many bureaucracies are characterized by a great deal of structural looseness; rules are not always formulated in highly specific terms, and policies are often adjusted to accommodate diversity. Kohn (1971) noted that bureaucratic organizations can offer challenge, job protection, and rewards, and often attract persons with a high level of education. Consequently, he found that employees of large, centralized organizations were more flexible and receptive to change than workers in less bureaucratized ones.

Organizations often adapt themselves to the characteristics of their clientele. For example, schools in low-income neighborhoods often seem to place less stress on attendance, tardiness, and dress codes, and use corporal punishment more often than middle-class schools. Of course, such adaptions do not necessarily help clients. In many instances, they only work to the clients' disadvantage. Goal displacement, then, can result from either extreme, complete autonomy or co-optation by special interests. The key to effectiveness may be the kind of balance the organization is able to strike between these two extremes.

Probably enough has been said to demonstrate that citizen participation has important implications for a variety of issues. We have suggested a few and others have been raised in the first two volumes of this series. Therefore, we shall now turn to consider opportunities for citizens to participate in their local schools. As we proceed, it is important to keep

in mind two impinging features of the external environment in which schools exist, for they dictate what kind of governance is possible:
- The way school districts are organized sets definite limits on the amount of influence and surveillance local citizens can exercise;
- "Local" schools are part of a nationwide network of organizations that share in their governance.

Recent efforts to increase the participation of citizens, particularly disadvantaged citizens, have been preoccupied with administrative decentralization, neighborhood control, and related activities at the *local* level. We shall take the position that these efforts can at best be only partially successful for two reasons. First, there are serious structural impediments to citizen participation at the local level, and second, and perhaps more important, schools are governed by *national* coalitions of organizations and "veto" groups beyond the local level. We shall develop both themes in the following discussions.

Some Limitations Of School Boards

To understand the citizen participation movement, it is necessary to start with the local school board. It is one of the few institutions that holds out to citizens the *promise* of a real opportunity to participate in a vital public service. However, in practice school boards have failed to effectively represent large segments of citizens. First, they do not represent a full cross section of the local citizenry. There is a widely acknowledged pattern of oligarchical rule in local school districts. While a large proportion of the constituency of American schools is poor, schools are governed primarily by upper-middle class, propertied, monied, white, middle-aged Republican men. Hottlemen (1973) echoes many other writers when he concludes that:

> There is enough evidence available to demonstrate that school board governance, broadly speaking, has long been a system dominated by a narrow range of citizens. One can only speculate about the degree of self-interest which permeates decisions made about the future of children, but it is difficult not to believe that unenlightened self-interest has been a key element in the motivation for school board service.

Second, school board members typically are unable to represent even their own segment of the community effectively. The reason is that they generally do not play a decisive role in making policy decisions, ironic though that may seem. There are several reasons to explain their lack of power. Board members usually hold demanding, full-time jobs which limit the amount of time they can spend on school matters; they do not use objective data to evaluate their superintendents and their schools; they usually do not run on a specific platform, and thus do not have a mandate from the community to act in any particular way; and they do not represent any group or special constituency and for that reason do not report back to a constituency (even when they are elected from subdistricts of the larger school district).

This last point is crucial. School board members usually do not represent visible constituencies who back them in elections and monitor their performance, and only rarely are clear *issues* involved in school board elections. As a result, new members are allowed freedom to adjust to the expectations of administrators and senior board members. One reason constituencies often fail to materialize is that members are so uniformly upper class and, therefore, do not represent issues uniquely important to other groups. Another reason is that public disagreement and a wide variety of parental interests tend to cloud the emergence of clear issues and/or answers regarding the school program.

By comparison to school boards, school superintendents have a considerable amount of power because they have full-time jobs, control the agenda for board meetings, are specialists in their field, have specialized staff persons working for them, control many aspects of the organization of the school system, define alternatives for the board, produce their own research and thereby control the information available to board members, make specific policy recommendations, and are in charge of hiring, assignment, promotion, and tenure.

As a result, school boards are often co-opted by administrators. For example, they often champion proposals from the professional staff, rather than representing citizen groups. Moreover, at many board meetings the vast majority of the time is devoted to managerial details instead of policy issues.

It is perhaps ironic that there has been such widespread disenchantment and frustration with local school boards when one of the few places community residents appear to have a voice in public policy is through their school board. Perhaps it is precisely because schools hold out the promise of opportunities for citizen participation that people have been so disappointed with the results. In any case, these inadequacies of school boards have stirred a great deal of criticism and have provided the impetus behind many serious experiments in recent years to explore ways for citizens to participate more effectively in the governance of schools. Perhaps school boards need to look again at ways in which citizens can contribute to their deliberations and should explore other means of checking with their constituents before they take action.

The Many Meanings of Citizen Participation

The solutions proposed create their own problems. For example, we have already alluded to the efforts being made to include citizens more directly in the governance process. One of the major problems with such moves is that people have different understandings about how citizens can and should participate. One way to approach this issue is to consider what it would require for citizens to be fully *effective* in their efforts to make themselves heard, even though some people might object to so much outside influence.

CITIZEN EFFECTIVENESS DEFINED

For our immediate purposes, we shall define effective citizen participation as *the ability of organized citizen groups (a) to obtain recognition as legitimate spokespersons for their constituencies and (b) to achieve their objectives with respect to the educational program.* Of course there can be various degrees of effectiveness. Even if a group does not prevail, it can be partially effective if its views are taken into account in any compromise that is reached.

We want to stress that we are considering only organized forms of citizen participation and that we are using the term "effectiveness" only as it applies to the ability of a citizen group to be heard and have its influence felt. Effectiveness in this sense should not be equated with effective governance of the system. We leave open the possibility that a school system will be governed no more effectively when citizens are successful in their efforts to be heard than when they are not. Our purpose is to reflect on what it means to say that citizens are effective in making themselves heard.

In choosing to approach the problem in this way, from the viewpoint of the citizen, we have also chosen to ignore the variety of individuals and groups that can be involved when citizens "participate" in schools. For example, from the community side there are individual parents, citizens without children in schools, elected or appointed community officials, informal leaders, ad hoc pressure groups, voters, and the students. From the side of the school district there are a school board, administrators, specialists and classroom teachers, teacher organizations, and assistants or secretaries at the central office and in the individual schools. Conceivably, each of these groups or individuals has a different idea about how citizens can effectively participate. However, given the complexity of the topic, it seems necessary to limit the discussion by focusing sharply on the conditions that influence the ability of citizen groups to make themselves heard.

As defined above, Gamson (1975) identifies two dimensions of citizen effectiveness: (a) acceptance, i.e. the group is recognized by officials as a valid representative for a legitimate set of interests; (b) impact, i.e. the group has gained benefits for its constituency.

Acceptance

A group can be accepted in a variety of ways depending upon the type of participation in which it engages, or the role it is expected to assume. Perhaps the most significant form of acceptance is being included in the decision-making process, though citizens can effectively be involved in other ways as well. Therefore, it would be useful to identify different types of roles open to citizens. Here is one framework for thinking about citizen roles:

THE CLIENT ROLE. Here, the citizen group asks for assistance or advice from the school district regarding specified problems. This assumes that citizens are aware of problems and will initiate the relationship. The school or district then reserves the right to determine if the request is legitimate and when and how it will respond to the request.

THE CONSULTANT ROLE. In this case, the relationship is reversed. That is, the school or school district seeks advice from the citizen group. The group is asked to act in a consulting capacity. But there are many different forms of consulting. Citizens may be asked to serve in a "sounding out" role; for example, to appraise for the school board a new sex education program that is being contemplated. Or they may serve in a "review" capacity to re-examine the curriculum of an elementary school or evaluate a grading policy. Or, they may be directed to "explore" a particular question such as what should be done about work-study programs, environmental education, or adding a multicultural dimension to the school program. Low-income parents might be convened to explore how the home can complement the school in the reading program or how a school breakfast and lunch program can involve parents so that good nutrition is practiced at home. Finally, other aspects of consulting include "fact-finding," "analysis," or "interpretation." For example, the group may be asked to survey members of the community to ascertain public opinion on an issue; it may be asked to explain neighborhood traditions and ethnic values to school officials; or it may be asked to explain the reason for a certain event, such as why a school bond levy was defeated. In any case, citizens acting as consultants may be expected to perform one or more of at least three functions: (a) to provide information, (b) to interpret events and give solicited advice, and (c) to help support and legitimize the district's actions.

THE DECISION-MAKER ROLE. In this role, the group is invited to participate formally in the decision-making process through permanent or ad hoc committees and special assignments. It may participate in only one decision or in several. It may participate at the level of the district and/or at the level of specific schools. Citizens may have a high percentage of representatives or only a few.

THE IMPLEMENTOR ROLE. The school or school district is the initiator in this role also. The group is called upon to collaborate in implementing existing policy or procedure (e.g., to assist with fund raising campaigns or to provide volunteer aids).

THE CONSUMER ROLE. Again, under this definition, the school or school district takes the initiative. The citizen group is treated as a passive consumer. Through the mass media, speeches, telephone calls and personal visits, school officials initiate many communications with citizens to inform and persuade them of the school problems (from the officials' viewpoint).

Impact

The opportunity for a group to participate, of course, does not assure that it will have any influence on a school's practices. Therefore, it is necessary to consider what advantages a group may have gained for its constituency, that is the number of requests or demands for which it has gained modest or large concessions. In weighing these advantages, it is necessary to assess several factors.

First, the advantage depends upon the point at which citizens enter the decision process, or the *type of participation*. The decision process can be divided in a number of ways. Here is one possibility:

- participation in specifying alternatives that are being considered;
- participation in choices among these alternatives;
- ascertaining what decisions need to be made;
- retaining control over the final approval or veto of decisions by others.

Second, the *scope of a group's involvement* must be taken into account. This can be assessed by the number of decision areas in which the group has participated, such as: subjects and programs; teaching materials; methods of reporting pupil progress; disciplinary methods; grouping of students; hiring and evaluation of teachers and administrators; allocations of budgets; policies governing street language and standard English; and ways to deal with absenteeism, drug abuse, vandalism, and disruptive behavior.

Third, the *domain of the decision* should be weighed, that is, its impact as reflected in the number of individuals and/or time or effort involved. For example, district-wide versus school-based concessions; the establishment of general hiring policies versus a decision to hire a specific elementary school principal; text book policy versus the veto of a specific book; homework policy versus a decision about a specific teacher's school work assignments. We hazard a guess that the smaller the context, the greater the domain of the citizens groups, assuming that authority is decentralized.

Finally, it is important to consider the *length and continuity of involvement,* in other words, the extent to which participation has been institutionalized. For example, a group might be centrally involved in making a particular decision, only to lose its influence after a short period of time. It might become involved intermittently only at crucial decision periods. Or, it might be involved, either in a central way or marginally, over a long period of time.

Forms of Participation

Citizen participation can take different forms (Thompson & McEwen, 1958; Corwin, 1965). The form it takes depends partly upon the relationship between the two dimensions discussed above, namely acceptance and impact.

Degree to which the Citizens' Group is Accepted by School	Degree of Impact of Citizens' Groups on Schools		
	High	Medium	Low
High	Passive Adaptation (of the school)	Coalition	Co-optation (by the school)
Medium	Bargaining		
Low	Conflict		

Figure 1. *Forms of citizen participation in educational decision making.*

Passive Adaptation in Figure 1 refers to the willingness of the school district to defer to a group in order to avoid any possibility of displeasing the group. It is a structural form of "ritualistic conformity." For example, a librarian might submit his/her book list to the American Legion for its approval; or, citizens might "bite the bullet" rather than openly criticize a teacher in order to avoid the remote possibility of "getting their child in trouble with the teacher." In these cases the school or citizens disagree with the goals but go along with the procedures.

Coalition is an open and mutually beneficial combination of a citizen group and a school district for a specific purpose such as organizing business-education week, reporting student progress, promoting cooperative education programs, or facilitating the consolidation of school districts. In these cases it is assumed that there is no basic disagreement on the goals and the means to be used.

Co-optation occurs when an organization links itself with a group whose name is then used as a "front" to legitimate a school district policy over which the group has, in reality, little influence. Typically, co-optation is accomplished when an organization absorbs the leadership of an opposing group into its own leadership. For example, in a study of the Tennessee Valley Authority, Selznick (1949) described a federal agency which was able to neutralize strong public opposition by appointing representatives of the hostile groups to its own governing board. For an example closer to schools, school administrators sometimes try to silence vocal critics by appointing them to citizen advisory committees. Some studies indicate that local Parent Teacher Associations (PTA) are sometimes used as fronts by school principals to support a pet program. For example, a principal might submit a controversial program to the school board in the name of the PTA in the belief that school boards will be reluctant to oppose parents (Sykes, 1953).

Bargaining occurs when a citizen group and school officials openly recognize that they do not share the same objectives, but remain ready to compromise in order to gain some advantage.

Conflict occurs when school officials overtly resist the claims or demands of an outside group. If a third party, such as a court or state legislature, intervenes, and the two parties no longer confront one another directly, the conflict has been changed into a form of competition.

THE DYNAMICS OF CITIZEN PARTICIPATION

The above range of possible citizen roles only begins to touch upon some of the complexities involved in citizen participation. For example, it is possible for several roles to be operating simultaneously in any one school district. More important, roles change over time. For example, a relationship that begins as a coalition can quickly evolve into co-optation; or bargaining can escalate into conflict. Two tendencies seem to be especially pervasive; (a) participation tends to become progressively selective, and (b) citizens tend to be co-opted by the organization.

Both tendencies are illustrated in a study of the "Mobilization for Youth" program in New York City (Helfgot, 1974). While the study doesn't directly concern schools, there are some parallels with obvious implications for citizen participation in schools. During the decade the program was in operation, there was a marked shift in leadership. Initially, the relatively poor, disadvantaged, indigenous members of the community constituted a large proportion of the governing board. They tended to be concerned about structural problems and, for example, wanted to work directly on discrimination in hiring policies and the unavailability of some services and resources to the poor. Then, over just a few short years, a new kind of leadership emerged consisting of well-educated minority groups who, in essence, were a kind of elite group. The indigenous, low-income residents of the local community were replaced by well-educated members from the same racial group who did not live in low-income areas. In effect, the poor were being symbolically represented by middle-class elites from the same minority group (see Figure 2). One reason for this shift is that the professional staff preferred to work with board members who would be sympathetic to their view and would defer to their expertise. By using minority elites in this way, the organization was able to strike a compromise between (a) pressures from the agency that funded the program to involve the poor in the governance of the program and (b) pressures from the professional staff who preferred to work with well-educated, middle-class people.

We do not mean to imply that these tendencies toward selective participation and co-optation are irrevocable. Indeed, the amount and form of citizen participation in a given school district depends to a great extent upon the way the district has been organized. This idea will be elaborated and developed below.

	Forms of Citizen Participation	
Segment of Community Represented	Clients, Consumers and Consultants	Decision Makers
Class and Residence	Traditional Social Service	Indigenous Influence
Race and Ethnicity	Small Voluntary Association	Symbolic Representation of the Poor

Figure 2. *Symbolic representation of the poor.* *

*Adapted from Helfgot, 1974.

Structural Impediments to Citizen Participation at the Local Level

We believe that citizen participation is related to two sets or kinds of organizational characteristics: characteristics of the citizen group and characteristics of the school district.

GROUP CHARACTERISTICS

Five types of characteristics of citizen groups should be considered: membership, leadership, solidarity, communication channels and the tactics used.

Membership Characteristics

Several aspects of membership composition can influence the group's effectiveness.

MEMBERSHIP BASE. First, the size and heterogeneity of the group can influence how effective it will be. The more members in the group and the more segments of the community it represents, the more persuasive its claim to be heard. In other words, legitimacy of the group (insofar as this is reflected in numbers) probably increases with its size and with the heterogeneity of its membership base.

Paradoxically, the same factors may reduce a group's ability to gain concessions, because both size and heterogeneity may promote factionalism and interfere with the group's ability to organize its members. Thus, a group's ability to make an impact might decline with its size and heterogeneity even though its acceptance may increase.

THE STATUS OF A GROUP'S MEMBERS. We make the assumption that the power of clients and their attitudes toward public agencies vary with their social class (see Azumi & Hage, 1972, p. 73). There is some evidence that higher-status clients tend to be more readily accepted and are more assertive in making demands on an organization than their lower-status counterparts (Katz & Danet, 1970). In addition, service organizations seem to prefer middle-class citizens as clients because their values and needs are compatible with the organization's procedures and goals. By contrast, the status difference between low-income citizens and middle-class educators minimizes the amount of interaction between them; indeed it seems that the larger the status difference, the less interaction required for the activity to go smoothly.

It seems likely, then, that groups comprised of the upper socioeconomic strata and those comprised of older persons and males, will be more readily accepted, and perhaps will also have more impact than groups with the opposite characteristics. As a result, lower-status clientele generally seem to get less attention and lower quality service from service organizations than higher-status clientele.

In addition to this social class factor, Katz and Danet (1966, 1973) found that the clients' prior experience with public bureaucracies made an important difference. Those with more experience in dealing with all types of public organizations seemed to be more effective in dealing with the organizations studied.

Another aspect of a group's status is the number of options it has available to obtain needed services from more than one source. It is difficult to mobilize citizens into action when the dissatisfied group has the option of leaving the system (Hirshman, 1970). If a group can withdraw its children from the local school and send them elsewhere it will be less inclined to make its voice heard by exerting pressure on the school.

In general then, we suggest that the effectiveness of a citizen group increases with the proportion of its members from the higher social class and diminishes with the alternatives available to its members to obtain the services they want from a competing source.

Leadership Characteristics

Another question is whether citizen groups that permit extensive participation within the group are more effective than those which rely on a few elite leaders. Again, factors that promote a group's acceptance do not guarantee that it can influence decisions. For example, it seems to us that acceptance will increase *if:* leaders are elected by members in frequent elections, and with large voter turnouts; there is a broad base of participation in policy decisions; the social characteristics of the leaders resemble those of the rank-and-file members.

However, such broad-based participation tends to produce divisiveness and reduce the group's ability to organize its members. The more of its members who have little education, low income, and little political power, the less leverage a group is likely to have. Therefore, an elite leadership might be able to gain more concessions than leaders drawn widely from the rank-and-file. In short, a group with an elite leadership structure might have difficulty gaining legitimacy either from its own members or from outsiders, but it often can be more influential than one which is completely democratic.

Group Solidarity

A group's acceptability and impact are also influenced by its internal solidarity. The ability to maintain a united front and to motivate members to work for group objectives are sources of strength. Groups can achieve solidarity in many different ways, including stringent membership criteria, strong, informal group pressures, an experienced membership, broad participation in the decision-making, and even-handed enforcement of clearly stated rules and policies.

Communication Channels

Another factor that may improve a group's ability to gain acceptance and to be heard is whether some of its members are specifically assigned to deal with different people in the school system. When there are people in "boundary roles" connecting the group with other such groups within and outside the community, the group can learn from and share experiences of other citizen groups. So, we expect that a group's ability to gain acceptance and influence decisions will increase with the number of specialized boundary positions responsible for interfacing with the school district and with other citizen groups.

Tactics

Finally, questions can be raised about the relative effectiveness of different types of tactics that a group may use. We are not prepared to classify such tactics or to assess their effectiveness, but they seem to range from pleas directed to school officials or to the public, and lobbying (either the school administration, the school board or some third party such as a legislative group), to direct confrontations. There are also differences in style of approach, ranging from subtle and smooth to hostile or belligerent. It should be noted, too, that there may be a good deal of informal influence by citizens related to a specific plan or revision suggested by a citizens' group or exercised by directing teachers and administrators to new or different ideas and programs.

SCHOOL DISTRICT CHARACTERISTICS

While the characteristics of citizen groups are important, they tell only part of the story. Features of the schools and school districts also play a vital role in determining how much opportunity citizens will have to participate in school governance. We see two dimensions of school districts that can buffer educators from the citizens they serve: mechanisms of administrative control, and peer pressures of colleagues. Indeed, it is probably impossible to increase citizen participation at the local level without making some changes in both types of characteristics.

Administrative Controls

We suggest that bureaucratic characteristics discourage employees from interacting with the public and encourage them to treat citizens impersonally. Organizations that are rigidly controlled promote conformity to the rules and to the authority system instead of encouraging employees to be responsive to the public. Conversely, when there is less stress on bureaucratic characteristics, employees have more opportunity to meet the public and relate to them on a personalized basis. We shall elaborate by considering several bureaucratic characteristics (see Corwin & Wagenaar, 1977).

FORMALIZATION. Rigid enforcement of rules encourages employees to behave in impersonal ways toward outsiders. If there are clear rules covering a situation, there is little need for personal discussions with clients when problems arise; they can be referred to the rule. Rules also can protect employees from outside requests they may consider inconvenient or inappropriate (Bar-Yosef & Schild, 1966). For example, if a parent requests that his/her child be assigned to a specific teacher, the principal need only send a note or form letter describing the procedures used in making random assignments which in effect prohibit special requests. The more rigidly such rules and procedures are enforced, the less subject the principal will be to outside pressures. For these reasons, rules help to maintain social distance between organizations and their clients.

However, rules also increase the likelihood that there will be difficulty with those citizens who do not understand or subscribe to them. They promote tension between the organization and its clientele.

We conclude that citizen groups will have more difficulty gaining acceptance and having an impact in districts that are more formalized in comparison to those that are less formalized.

CENTRALIZATION. Centralization tends to insulate lower echelon employees from public contact, because they must refer citizens to higher levels where the final decision about their problems will be made. Employees can then disclaim responsibilities for the policies and decisions opposed by citizens. Conversely, decentralized organizations are likely to be more open to citizens, who then can go directly to a variety of decision points for answers. Subordinates in decentralized organizations have more discretion to respond to citizens' requests on an individual basis. Therefore, citizens' groups will usually have a better chance to gain acceptance in districts that are decentralized in comparison to those that are more centralized.

Of course, gaining access to the organization does not assure that the citizens will get their way. This depends upon the type of concessions they seek. Indeed, it may be more difficult to win some types of concessions in decentralized districts than in centralized ones. The reader may wish to speculate further on this.

SENIORITY. The experience of employees, or their longevity in the school or school district, will also affect the way they identify with local citizens. Experience can have two very different effects. Over time an employee will associate with members of the public on more and more occasions. In the process the person is likely to become identified with certain individuals in the community and perhaps will become sensitive to their wishes. But at the same time, as a member of the organization, that employee will probably also begin to place more value on organizational norms. After a period of years the individual may become preoccupied with organizational security and power at the expense of the clientele, or after some point, may simply lose interest (Blau, 1960). So, we expect that seniority is an important factor that operates in a rather complex way to affect the ability of citizen groups to gain acceptance and exert influence.

Work Group Controls

The attitudes of professional employees toward members of the public are shaped by the opinions of their colleagues. These collegial norms can be enforced through (a) active teacher and/or administrator organizations, and (b) formal training or socialization into the profession.

PARTICIPATION IN PROFESSIONAL ORGANIZATIONS. Work organizations often amass power. The way that power is used is as important as the fact that professionals have it. On the one hand, strong work-group organizations give employees some leverage over the bureaucracy, i.e., some autonomy to protect the client from its worst features. On the other hand, this same power can be used to protect and insulate professionals from the public, in the belief that citizens do not have the necessary expertise and often want special favors.

In one respect at least, the control exercised by work organizations is analogous to administrative controls: both can protect employees from the personal demands made by the members of the public. When teachers can turn to their organizations for backing, they are not likely to be easily intimidated by persons requesting personal favors. They are in an even better position to remain objective and impersonal toward things like grading, which often arouse strong feelings in parents. There is some evidence to support this. Studies have found that employees who belong to cohesive work groups act more impersonally toward their clients than employees who do not. They are also less likely to conform to clients' expectations and more likely to uphold organizational norms when there is a conflict. (Blau & Scott, 1962, p. 108; Wagenaar, 1974; Bar-Yosef & Schild, 1966). These studies support the general proposition that when an occupational group has reason to be suspicious of outsiders, it will interact less frequently with them.

All of these reasons suggest that citizens' groups will have less direct impact where the school district has strong teacher organizations than where teachers are not so active. However, there is also another possibility. It is possible that where a system has been organized and where collective bargaining is used those who disagree with one another will have more opportunity to resolve their differences. Parents perhaps find it easier to be heard when there is opportunity for them to negotiate and when there are people skilled in bargaining to whom they can turn. In comparison, they will have more difficulty in finding representation in less militant school districts where there are fewer avenues and mechanisms for resolving disagreement.

FORMAL TRAINING. Ideally, advanced training at a good college or university should instill in professional employees a service ethic and the necessary competence to work closely with the public. However, in practice most professions have been widely criticized for being too socially distant and unresponsive to citizens, most especially to low-income clients. As noted, the fact that teachers have been socialized into a distinct occupational subculture produces a "cultural gap" between them and their public. Moreover, teachers in a local school often look to their associates from other communities for advice. They may be more influenced by their professional colleagues in other places than by people in their immediate school districts. The better-trained teachers have more opportunity to escape problem-ridden, low-income communities and gravitate to the more stable communities where perhaps there is less need to interact with the public because there are fewer problems to deal with.

In other words, citizens' groups often have difficulty gaining acceptance and being heard in schools where the staff has a strong sense of professionalism and high levels of formal training. Still, this is not inevitable and often depends on the quality of local professional leadership and the way they use power. Preservice and inservice training programs could be designed to help sensitize teachers to the irony that in the process of becoming technically more competent, they might tend to become less sensitive to the public they serve. Because collective organizations give them protection, teachers could avoid the predicament by daring to violate some of the long-standing prejudices and traditions against working closely with families in poor neighborhoods. Teacher organizations could even insist upon participation in training programs that would better equip teachers to deal with low-income children and adults who have lifestyles, values, and behavior patterns different from their own.

OTHER CONSIDERATIONS

In addition to the characteristics of the citizens' groups and school districts considered thus far, other important features of the larger social context deserve mention.

Composition of the Governing Board

Crain (1968) found from a case study of 15 cities that the crucial variable affecting the decision to desegregate school systems was the composition of the school board, in particular, members' political liberalism, and whether they were elected or appointed. Elected and politically liberal board members had a positive effect on desegregation. Moreover, he concluded that civil rights demonstrations and other direct pressures had relatively little effect on what the boards did.

Age of the Organization

It is perhaps easier for an organization to defend its boundaries if it has been in existence for some time. In his discussion of the "liabilities of newness," Stinchcombe (1965) makes the point that new or insecure organizations may be more inclined than older, secure ones to appeal to clients by holding out the opportunity for participation or influence. The need to attract new clients also might foster a service credo.

Turnover of Personnel

Sometimes organizations become more responsive to outside pressure because of turnover of personnel, especially at the executive level. A number of studies have suggested that organizations in which there has been a succession of leadership from outside the organization undergo more change (and hence can be more responsive to new client demands) than organizations in which insiders are promoted to positions of leadership. Carlson (1962) found that when school boards actively sought new superintendents from outside the school district, the board was already dissatisfied with the system and authorized a new leader to make changes.

Prestige of the Organization

An organization's prestige in the local community also might influence its relationship with the public. Acquiring a "favorable image" represents one way of gaining power relative to clients. Caplow (1964) notes that the prestige system in which organizations establish standards and procedures are then emulated by other organizations in the set. This prestige hierarchy can minimize the ability of organizations to respond to citizens' demands.

Prestige considerations compound the difficulties of dealing with lower-class citizens. In general, in an organization that has high status, the members who rank *low* within it tend to be insecure in dealing with leaders from less prestigious organizations. This is because the status of low-ranking people in high-status organizations is marginal, and hence will cause these people to be anxious to avoid contacts with members of a low prestige group whose association with them might cast further doubt upon their status. They will be at a particular disadvantage when dealing with leaders from such groups who have more internal power than they have in their own organization. Caplow (1964) suggests that both "low persons in high groups" and "high persons in low groups," being subject to status inconsistencies when they interact with one another, tend to isolate themselves from such contacts as circumstances permit.

Organizational Scale

Evidence indicates that as the size of an organization increases so does social distance, and unresponsiveness to the public (Etzioni, 1964). There seem to be two reasons for this. First, larger organizations tend to draw a wider variety of clients. Because of this, the organization is not dependent upon any one group of clients, and no one group can exert much leverage over the organization. Second, larger organizations tend to be more formal, especially because they must use impersonal technologies to process large numbers of clients. Consequently it is difficult for them to maintain intensive relationships with the public.

Larger organizations also tend to use formal protocol in decision making because they are more remote from the members. For example, members of a state board of education usually deal with questions and decisions rather formally, partly because of the remoteness of the state level activity to the local and more intimate situations, but also because they are in a more public arena and under the scrutiny of a much larger and more diverse constituency.

Private Versus Public Control

The fact that public schools have a virtual monopoly over the education of most pupils and face relatively little competition provides them with a form of security which engenders insulation from public pressure. Whereas competition introduces some uncertainty which can force an organization to adapt to changes, absence of competitors permits the organization to be impervious to social changes (Thompson, 1967).

Carlson (1964) contrasts public schools with what he calls "wild" organizations which must compete for clientele and resources. Public schools are "domesticated" in the sense that they are guaranteed to have clients and a minimum of necessary resources, and their funds are not tied closely to measures of the quality of their performance. He suggests that domesticated organizations like school systems, because they are protected, are slower to change and less willing to adapt than are wild organizations.

However, political pressure can sometimes compensate for the absence of competition. There has been a considerable amount of political pressure on service organizations to become more responsive to citizens. Although legislatures and public officials represent an Anglo-upper-social stratum, the federal government has taken an active interest in providing aid to low-income, ethnic class people. The Morrill Act, Title I and Title III, and civil rights legislation of the 1965 Education Act, have added provisions for deprived people such as minorities and women.

Cultural and Contextual Variations

The culture of a nation can also influence the opportunities available for citizen participation. Because there has been little support for cross-national research on this topic, very little is known about it. However, we can offer a few conjectures. The extent to which citizens honor professional training, feel the need for professional services, and believe that skill rather than political criteria should govern bureaucratic policy is likely to vary within and across nations (Stimson & LeBelle, 1971). Crozier (1964) concluded that the French culture contributed to the impersonal, highly centralized French bureaucracy in which subordinates accepted little responsibility. Presthus (1959) found that the overriding social values in Turkey produced what he calls a "welfare bureaucracy," in which the importance of hiring the unemployed is placed above the Western preference for efficiency.

Societal values and structure have been used to explain differences between organizations with the same goals. Vaughan and Archer (1971) have pointed out that, historically, the English and French school systems developed divergent forms of organization. In Britain by the mid-19th century, education remained voluntary, decentralized, unintegrated, unspecialized, and unstandardized, while in France it became fully bureaucratized and state controlled. They attribute the difference to the degree of success that various organized groups had in challenging the dominance of the church. In England, the middle class solicited voluntary funds to establish alternative institutions. In France the bourgeoisie used its influence with revolutionary legislative assemblies to enact legislation replacing the church; education became rationalized following the triumph of administrative bureaucratization throughout the state. For a number of reasons, administrative decentralization in England seems to have led to greater autonomy for teachers, whereas in the United States it has led to less. Mole (1974) has updated this comparative analysis and extended it to more recent time.

Turbulence in the Environment

An environment that is (a) *heterogeneous* and populated by diverse types of people or economic activities, and (b) *dynamic* in the sense of containing many people who are geographically or socially mobile, is referred to as "turbulent" (Terreberry, 1968). An organization in a turbulent environment will be under pressure to be responsive to the changing goals and interests of its clientele. One way that organizations cope with turbulent environments is to segment themselves into separate units; since any group of employees has only a limited span of surveillance and competence, this enables each unit to specialize in dealing with a particular segment of the outside environment. For this reason, the more turbulent the environment, the more complex and decentralized the organization is likely to become (Thompson, 1967). Public school systems, for example, divided themselves into elementary and secondary schools and are usually graded internally, which is one way of adapting to the different interests or demands of a unique clientele. However, when organizations attempt to maintain standardized procedures and a centralized decision-making process in turbulent environments, it is predictable that there will be strain between the organization and the public.

These, then, are some of the major features of citizens' groups, school districts and their contexts that can affect their openness to, or isolation from, local citizens. Any effort to increase citizen participation cannot be fully successful unless such factors are taken into consideration and, where necessary and possible, altered.

The Limits of Local Control
Over Education, Section II:

NATIONAL NETWORKS OF CONTROL

To this point we have concentrated on the opportunity that citizens have to participate in the affairs of their local schools. And, it is clear that—although the degree of participation varies depending upon the circumstances—there are some formidable obstacles to citizen participation at this level. But we now come to an even more important consideration. Indeed, to the extent that it is thought desirable to have more citizen participation, we have barely scratched the surface of the problem. For many of the most crucial decisions about local schools are controlled *outside* local communities at the state, regional, and national centers of power, which impose standards binding on local educators but which are virtually inaccessible to citizens through the community channels considered thus far (see Wayland, 1964).

Because local school boards are prominent in most communities, and because the issues that come before local boards sometimes receive extensive publicity, it is easy to overestimate the extent to which schools in this country are controlled at the local level. But in reality, much of the time and energy of local boards is devoted to implementing, or reacting to, decisions made elsewhere—the local, state and federal legislative bodies and agencies, the courts, and a wide array of nongovernmental (or quasi-governmental) organizations and groups. Some of the principal organizations involved are listed in Figure 3, together with illustrations of types of decision areas that they can affect.

Clark's (1965) observation provides a succinct description of the form of governance that is emerging in education:

> There is some shift upward in the formal locus of educational decision making, from the local to state level in public education, and from local and state to the national level . . . . But much of the change taking place is in arrangements that lie in part outside the hierarchy of public offices . . . . The emerging patterns depend on voluntary relations among public agencies and private groups. In some degree, these arrangements serve as substitutes for or as alternatives to formal internal administration, that is, to the national-state-local line of ministerial authority found in many countries. The patterns represent ways of influencing the grass-roots level of operation in a field where no formal authority can impose cooperation.

These interorganizational patterns, or confederations, constitute an alternative to traditional public bureaucracy. Bureaucracy relies upon formalization, personnel assignment and review, Research and Development (R&D), rational decision making, and other mechanisms discussed

	Type of Authority	Area Affected
Decision Areas Controlled or Affected	Laws and Regulations / Policy / Budgets and Funds / Program Approval or Control	Teacher Preparation / Teacher Certification and Licensing / Attendance / School District Boundaries / Hiring Policies/Promotions / Racial Integration Practices / Attendance Requirements / Approvals and/or Adoptions of Texts and other Materials / Programs / Buildings
Types of Organizations and Groups Involved		
Federal Congress Federal Agencies		
Federal, State and Local Courts		
National Professional Associations		
National Accrediting Agencies		
Regional Accrediting Agencies		
State Legislatures Lobbying Groups Hearing Committees State Advisory Groups		
State Departments of Education Consultants Advisory Committees		
Teacher Training Institutions Deans of Education Professional Associations of College Professors		
Teacher (and Administrator) Organizations		
Accrediting Agencies Examination Boards Textbook Publishers		

Figure 3. *Types of organizations and groups involved in the governance of schools.*

in Volumes I and II. By contrast, confederations substitute implicit divisions of labor, subcontracting, temporary, voluntary alliances, dissemination, and the use of leverage via influence and exchanges of resources, prestige and service.

Although the general point we are making is probably clear, the overwhelming implications can be seen better as one considers the wide range of specific decision areas controlled or affected by some of the major organizations listed in Figure 3. For purposes of illustration, let's briefly inventory the powers of a few organizations, namely: federal agencies and the courts, state departments of education, teacher organizations, and accrediting agencies.

Federal Agencies and the Courts

The influence of federal legislation in education was first felt in the act of 1862 leading to the establishment of the land-grant colleges, then the Smith-Hughes Act of 1917 to stimulate vocational education, and after that the National Defense Education Act of 1958 to encourage the study of science and foreign languages, and finally, the legislation of the 1960's to aid handicapped children and to improve the education of low income children. In these instances the federal government did not issue orders directly to local school districts but instead offered money for specific areas of education which local districts could accept or reject.

Nevertheless, considering the narrow base of local funding (property tax) many school districts have had little choice except to abide by federal mandates in order to take advantage of federal money which is often needed to maintain schools at an acceptable level of quality. And more recently, the United States Office of Education (USOE) responding to court decisions and federal legislation, has intervened directly and decisively to control certain areas of local education. The most notable example is its efforts to enforce federal desegregation guidelines under the threat of both court action and withdrawing federal funds from local school districts.

National Council for the Accreditation of Teacher Education

The National Council for the Accreditation of Teacher Education (NCATE) is the officially approved agency for voluntary accreditation of teacher education in the United States. The members of the council are appointed by constituent groups of the teaching profession: teacher educators by the American Association of Colleges for Teacher Education (AACTE), teachers by the National Education Association (NEA), state department personnel by the National Association of State Directors of Teacher Education and Certification (NASDTEC), the Council of Chief State School Officers (CCSSO), the National School Boards Association (NSBA), and the Council for Exceptional Children (CEC), the National Association of School Psychologists (NASP), National Council for Teachers of Mathematics (NCTM), and Student National Education Association (SNEA).

The council through its accreditation powers bestows upon colleges and universities an indicator of quality for both undergraduate and graduate teacher education programs. Although accreditation is voluntary (a

VOTING MEMBERS

AACTE	8	CCSSO	1	NASP	1
NEA	8	NSBA	1	NCTM	1
NASDTEC	1	CEC	1	SNEA	1

ASSOCIATE MEMBERS
(No Vote)

Association for Educational Communications and Technology

National Council for the Social Studies

American Association of School Administrators

Association for Teacher Educators

Figure 4. *Representatives to NCATE.*

college must apply for accreditation), the power of the council is substantial, both real and psychological. For example, any college seeking national accreditation must first submit to an examination by a regional accrediting agency. It must prepare an institutional report that satisfies NCATE standards. It must stand the expense of transporting to campus and caring for a visiting team for several days, and risk the ignominy of failing to achieve accreditation. In responding to NCATE standards a college in some way conforms or subscribes to external requirements, to the generalized values of the teacher education community. The power of the council is also psychological. There is an aura of the elite among colleges in the accredited group. NCATE accreditation is listed in college catalogues. It is reported to legislatures, in the case of public colleges, and to governing boards of the institutions. School administrators are pressured by teacher organizations to hire only graduates of NCATE accredited institutions.

The NCATE also influences state departments of education, who themselves conduct a kind of accreditation, usually called state approval. Such influence touches both the substantive standards or criteria used in accrediting or approving and the process of accreditation.

The power of NCATE is variable, however. Some prestigious institutions actually frown upon NCATE. They consider their own standards and programs to be superior to NCATE requirements and think their institution benefits little or not at all from national accreditation. Some such institutions have threatened to withdraw from membership and two have in recent years withdrawn from NCATE. Such institutions either fail to understand the full power of NCATE as an arm of the profession to hurt their reputations and to ostrasize them and their graduates, or they think they can survive without acceding to procedures they find unhelpful. It could be argued that such institutions choose to defy rather than support standards of the profession at large. What is illustrated is a kind of institutional class system. A few universities with prestige, money, and reputation attempt to create a new, more elite social system—thinking they have the power to legitimize such status. What is yet to be seen is whether the profession at large and organizations within the profession will permit such rejection. It is conceivable that the profession might have power to force high prestige institutions to conform if they want to secure other needed support of the profession.

In the powerful institutions NCATE has been used by deans as leverage with governing boards and legislatures to secure buildings, faculty, or other resources. Some powerful deans have co-opted NCATE to get institutional evaluations that suit their own purposes.

Power plays are not restricted to external NCATE activities. Over the years the internal struggles of the council reflect the rise and fall of power groups (organizations) that make up or monitor NCATE. In the 1960's the National Commission on Accrediting (NCA), the governing body of all professional accrediting, warned the NCATE that its makeup should reflect stronger control by higher education, and to maintain their good standing with NCA, the council changed its membership and constitution to give higher education greater sway. In the 1970's the NEA has wielded power to increase the representation of practitioners on the council equal to that of higher education. The shift in power within NCATE between higher education and teacher groups seems a precursor to a political balance of power that is now beginning to spread to state-level activities. The power balance in both certification and inservice education has begun to shift. The topic leads us very nicely into the next discussion of state departments of education.

State Departments of Education

Each state has among its government bureaus a department of education (SDE). These are legally constituted agencies, usually the secretariat of the state board of education, that have responsibility for the state system of education. SDE's are responsible for monitoring, coordinating, facilitating, and administering sundry education activities. These usually include setting and monitoring standards for curriculum, teachers, physical plant, administration, and materials used in public schools. Sometimes there are requirements set for private schools. Perhaps most important, SDE's through state boards of education and legislatures have control of state funds to support local schools.

Although there are many similarities among departments of education in the separate states, there are also many differences. The range in salary of the chief state school officer, usually known as the superintendent of public instruction or the commissioner of education, runs from $20,000 to $60,000. Some chiefs are elected. Some are appointed by the governor. Among those elected some run on partisan tickets; others run without party designation.

Below the top level of SDE personnel, professional and support employees are protected by civil service, so there can be considerable continuity of program even when the chief officer and the immediate staff change. Consequently, in most states there is stability in SDE. Some critics complain about too much stability and the lethargy of bureaucracy. Bureaucrats in SDE's are often career people who wield considerable power and have command of substantial funds to influence state and local programs. Federal funds have contributed significantly to such power and influence, even though a great deal of federal money is "flow-through" funds, attainable by filling out the appropriate forms.

SDE's have legal power and in this important respect, differ from a voluntary organization like the NCATE. They also have some distinct limits in that they must conform to state government policy. Some of these policies are reasonable and appropriate, but some aspects are not designed for human services activities and detract greatly from the state department's efficiency and effectiveness. For example, state standards may be appropriate for motor vehicles or a bureau of standards, but prove too prescriptive for textbooks and curriculum. Mandated uniformity in teaching may detract from creativity and effective teaching of individual students, whereas uniformity in weight measures, safety requirements for automobiles, and traffic regulations are essential for the public welfare. Fortunately, SDE's and the teaching profession have succeeded in reducing many state requirements for uniformity for required courses and textbooks. But, of late, the imposition of new requirements for achievement and accountability seem to deny much of what was learned earlier about the desirability of diversity—learned most notably in the Eight Year Study.

The style of leadership in SDE's varies greatly—running the gamut from highly authoritarian to very democratic operations. Whatever the style of leadership, it usually can be recognized as a result of the state's history and traditions. The SDE's tend to reflect the culture of which they are a part. Power, for example, is used very differently by various SDE's. In some states it is clearly power *over;* directives come down from the state department and they are obeyed without much question. In other states policy is developed with a great deal of involvement by professionals in the field. The concept of collaboration, as an example, has very different operational meanings depending on the state in which it is being used.

Teacher Organizations

Teachers' associations and unions are other organizations that have influence in education. The activities and roles of teacher groups at the local level are well known in states that have laws providing for collective bargaining. Teachers have bargained effectively for salaries, fringe benefits, and better working conditions. In states where such goals have been achieved, of course bargaining continues and salary and other demands are still very much the subject of negotiation, but other aspects of professional activity and service are on the table, e.g., decision-making perogatives, policy matters, inservice education, assignment of teachers, etc.

Less well known among teacher organization activities are lobbying at the state legislature, political action programs to elect candidates or to promote causes (for example the Equal Rights Amendment), and participation in professional and lay advisory, policy and governing groups. Teachers are not only organized to promote their own purposes, to protect their members from unfair or capricious actions, and to ensure due process, they are also organized to further professionalize teaching by influencing standards of preparation and licensure, by participating in and supporting national accreditations (NCATE), by influencing legislation for inservice education, curriculum improvement, research, and a host of other professional matters.

Since both teacher associations and unions have essentially the same aggressive and vital programs, designed to assert and support teacher causes and convictions, it is not necessary to distinguish between the NEA and the American Federation of Teachers (AFT) in terms of style or approach. Teacher organizations represent nearly 2.5 million teachers. This large membership base gives them power—power with legislatures, state and national, and power in most deliberative bodies where education matters are discussed. The phenomenon of power is new for teacher organizations and it is new for the traditional power figures who have to reckon with the teachers. There is some evidence that neither group is yet quite accustomed to teachers having power and there is yet the question as to how much power there is and how it will be used. The former may be dependent on the latter—that is, how teachers use power may, in part, determine how much they obtain.

As yet the power of teachers through their organizations is a vital and dynamic phenomenon. The development of strong teacher organizations has occurred so rapidly that shifts in power structures have been more visible than they usually are. For example, the assertion of teacher power in demanding more influence in decisions about teacher training is evident in the establishment in more than 15 states of standards and licensure commissions or boards. The political persuasion exerted by teachers to obtain federal legislation to fund teacher centers is another illustration of teacher power in recent actions.

Teacher power is psychological as well as real. In positive ways that fact is illustrated by the recent creation of decision making and advisory committees and boards that include a majority of teachers. The precedent established in the teacher center legislation of a teacher majority on teacher center policy boards got quickly and voluntarily transferred to other governing groups. If not psychological power, this is certainly psychological momentum.

Having said what we have about various groups and organizations and the power and/or authority they have in influencing education, it should also be recognized that some of the same people make up different groups—some of which have rather different goals. For example, teachers are employees of a school district, faculty members in a particular school, members of teacher organizations, and citizens of a community. They may also be school board members and members of official or quasi-legal groups at the state and national level. So the view of the organizations that various people belong to cannot be simplified to suggest that we merely have one group in conflict or contention with another. We may, indeed, have groups in contention but they are not entirely separate and distinct. They are often groups of people in different roles who understand the ambivalence of being on both sides of a question—but ultimately have to make a decision. There is no clean way to separate citizens from bureaucrats or professionals or administrators because in one sense all are citizens and share in citizens' purposes.

Implications

Probably no ideology concerning the public schools in this country is more firmly entrenched than the notion that they are, and should be, controlled by local communities. This, of course, is not an entirely erroneous belief, because certainly important decisions about both policy and practice are strongly influenced, if not controlled at the local level. However, at best, local communities must *share* the governance of their schools with many groups at all levels of government and in the private sector. The importance of any increase in citizen participation at the local level must be weighed against this larger balance of power.

In effect, schools are subject to many competing sources of authority, each of which justifies the right of various groups to influence schools in different ways. There is the *traditional* authority of local communities, the *expert* authority of professional educators at all levels of government, the *legal* authority supporting the power of government officials, legislatures and courts at all levels of government, and even *charismatic* authority seized upon by informal leaders who spring up from time to time. Thus, it seems that almost anyone can claim some formal "right" to control education. And, in addition, many groups are able to informally influence schools in nonlegitimate ways.

Given the complex web of power over local schools, it is misleading to speak as though there were a "power structure" controlling education in this country. While power structures probably exist in some communities, it seems generally more accurate to think of schools being governed by what Reisman (1950) calls *veto groups,* or in other words, a wide variety of groups at local, state, regional, and national levels, each of which has the necessary power to prevent public actions inimical to its interests, but only infrequently having enough power to initiate new actions. No public official can act unilaterally without placating some of these veto groups.

Such a balance of power produces its own ironies. On the one hand, no community, group of citizens, or educators can act unilaterally. But on the other hand, the fact that disputes frequently arise among the various veto groups increases the options available to school officials and/or particular local citizens' groups. These conflicts among citizens usually will be decided by school officials, or on occasion, by local citizens' groups which act aggressively and decisively to seize the opportunity.

This last point touches upon a very important principle that is often overlooked: The outside environment and organizational structure not only impose constraints on school districts; they also can be arranged to provide more options and new opportunities. We hope this series of volumes has helped the reader to appreciate the wide latitude of discretion often available to professional educators and citizens alike—and to become more sensitive to these opportunities to improve the education of young people.

REFERENCES

Azumi, Koya, & Hage, Jerald. *Organizational systems: A text-reader in the sociology of organizations.* Lexington, Mass.: D.C. Heath & Co., 1972.
Bar-Yosef, R., & Schild, E.O. Pressures and defenses in bureaucratic roles. *American Journal of Sociology.* May 1966, *71,* 665-673.
Blau, Peter M., & Scott, W. Richard. *Formal organizations.* San Francisco: Chandler, 1962.
Blau, Peter. Orientations toward clients in a public welfare agency. *Administrative Science Quarterly,* December 1960, *5,* 344-361.
Caplow, T. *Principles of organization.* New York: Harcourt, Brace & World, 1964.
Carlson, Richard O. Environmental constraints and organizational consequences: The public school and its clients. In D. E. Griffiths (Ed.), *Behavioral science and educational administration,* 63rd Yearbook of the National Society for the Study of Education, Part II. Chicago: University of Chicago Press, 1964, pp. 262-276.
Carlson, Richard O. *Executive succession and organization change: Place-bound and career-bound superintendents of schools.* University of Chicago: Midwest Administration Center, 1962.
Clark, B. R. Interorganizational patterns in education. *Administrative Science Quarterly,* 1965, *10,* 224-237.
Coleman, James. *Education and political development.* Princeton, N.J.: Princeton University Press, 1965.
Corwin, Ronald G. Patterns of federal-local relationships in education: A case study of the rural experimental schools program. Prepared for the National Institute of Education and ABT Associations, February 1, 1977, mimeographed.
Corwin, Ronald G. *A sociology of education.* New York: Appleton-Century-Crafts, 1965, pp. 391-416.
Corwin, Ronald G., & Schmit, Marilyn. Teachers in inner city schools: A survey of a large-city school system. *Education and Urban Society,* 2; Feb., 1970.
Corwin, Ronald G. and Theodore C. Wagenaar. Boundary interaction between service organizations and their publics: A study of teacher-parent relationships. *Social Forces,* December 1976, *55,* 471-492.
Crain, Robert. *Politics of school desegregation: Community structure and policy-making.* Chicago: Aldine, 1968.
Crozier, M. *The bureaucratic phenomenon.* Chicago: University of Chicago Press, 1964.
Etzioni, Amitai. *Modern organizations.* Englewood Cliffs, N.J.: Prentice-Hall, 1964.
Friedson, Eliot. Dominant professions, bureaucracy and client services. In William R. Rosengren & Mark Lefton (Eds.), *Organizations and clients.* Columbus, Ohio: Charles E. Merrill, 1970.
Gamson, William. *The strategy of social protest.* Homewood, Ill.: Dorsey Press, 1975.
Gouldner, A. W. Organizational analysis. In R. K. Merton, L. Bloom, & L. S. Cottrell, Jr. (Eds.), *Sociology today.* New York: Basic Books, 1959.
Hage, Jerald. An axiomatic theory of organizations. *Administrative Science Quarterly,* December 1965, *10,* 289-320.

Haug, M., & Sussman, M. B. Professional autonomy and the revolt of the client. *Social Problems,* 1969 *17,* 153-161.

Havighurst, Robert J. *The public schools of Chicago.* Chicago: Board of Education, 1964.

Helfgot, Joseph. Professional reform organizations and the symbolic representation of the poor. *American Sociological Review,* August 1974, *39,* 475-491.

Hirshman, Albert O. *Exit, voice and loyalty: Responses to decline in firms, organizations and states.* Cambridge, Mass.: Harvard University Press, 1970.

Hofstadter, Richard. Antitrust in America. *Commentary,* 1964, *38,* 47-53.

Hollingshead, August B. *Elmtown's youth.* New York: Wiley, 1949.

Homans, George C. *The human group.* New York: Harcourt, Brace, 1950.

Hottleman, Girard D. School boards: Moneyed men governing the poor. *The Massachusetts Teacher,* January 1973, *52.*

Katz, Fred E. The school as a complex social organization. *Harvard Educational Review,* Summer 1964, *34,* 428-455.

Katz, Elihu, & Danet, Brenda. Petitions and persuasive appeals: A study of official-client relations. *American Sociological Review,* December 1966, *31,* 811-822.

Katz, Elihu, & Danet, Brenda. *Bureaucracy and the public.* New York: Basic Books, 1972.

Kerr, Norman J. The school board as an agency of legitimation. *Sociology of Education,* Fall 1964, *38,* 34-59.

Kohn, Melvin L. Bureaucratic man: A portrait and an interpretation. *American Sociological Review,* 1971, *36,* 461-474.

Laski, Harold. Bureaucracy. *Encyclopedia of the social sciences, III.* New York: MacMillan, 1935.

Male, George. *The struggle for power: Who controls the schools in England and the United States.* Beverly Hills, Calif.: Sage Publications, 1974.

Marris, Paul, and Rein, M. *Dilemmas of social reform.* New York: Atherton, 1968.

Merton, Robert K. *Social theory and social structure.* Glencoe, Ill.: Free Press, 1957.

Michels, Robert. *Political parties.* Glencoe, Ill.: Free Press, 1949.

Moynihan, Daniel P. *Maximum feasible misunderstanding: Community action in the war on poverty.* Glencoe, Ill.: Free Press, 1969.

Perrow, Charles. *Organizational analysis: A sociological View.* Belmont, Calif.: Wadsworth Publishing Co., 1970.

Perrucci, Robert, and Pilisuk, Marc. Leaders and ruling elites: The inter-organizational bases of community power. *American Sociological Review,* December 1970, *35,* 1040-1056.

Presthus, Robert. The social basis of bureaucratic organizations. *Social Forces,* December 1959, *38,* 103-109.

Reisman, David, Glazer, Nathan, & Denney, Reuel. *The lonely crowd: A study of the changing American character.* Garden City, N.Y.: Doubleday and Co., 1956.

Rosengren, William R. The careers of clients and organizations. In William R. Rosengren & Mark Lefton (Eds.), *Organizations and clients: Essays in the sociology of service.* Columbus, Ohio: Charles E. Merrill, 1970.

Selznick, Phillip. *TVA and the grass roots.* Berkeley: University of California Press, 1949.

Sjoberg, Gideon, Brymer, Richard A., & Farris, Buford. Bureaucracy and the lower class. *Sociology and Social Research,* April 1966, *50,* 325-337.

Stimson, J., & LaBelle, T. J. The organizational climate of Paraguayan elementary schools: Rural-urban differentiations. *Education and Urban Society,* 1971, *3,* 333-349.

Stinchcombe, A. Social structure and organizations. In J. G. March (Ed.), *Handbook of organizations.* Chicago: Rand McNally, 1965, pp. 142-193.

Sykes, Gresham. The P.T.A. and parent-teacher conflict. *Harvard Educational Review,* Spring 1953, *23,* 86-92.

Terreberry, S. The evolution of administrative environments. *Administrative Science Quarterly,* 1968, *12,* 590-613.

Thompson, James D. *Organizations in action.* New York: McGraw-Hill, 1967.

Vaughan, Michalina, & Archer, Margaret S. *Social conflict and educational change in England and France 1789-1848.* London: Cambridge University Press, 1971.

Wagenaar, T. C. Activist professionals: The case of teachers. *Social Science Quarterly,* September 1974, *55,* 372-379.

Waller, Willard. *The sociology of teaching.* New York: Wiley, 1932.

Wayland, Sloan. Structural features of American education as basic factors in innovation. In M. Miles (Ed.), *Innovations in education.* New York: Teachers College Press, 1964.

Weber, Alfred. Bureaucracy and freedom. *Modern Review,* March-April 1948, *3-4,* 176-186.

Wirt, F. M., & Kirst, M. W. *The political web of American schools.* Boston: Little, Brown, 1972.
Zeigler, Harman. *The irony of democracy.* Belmont, Calif.: Wadsworth Publishing Co., 1972.

OTHER SUGGESTED READING

Abrahamsson, Bengt. *Bureaucracy or participation: The logic of organization.* Beverly Hills, Calif.: Sage Publications, 1977.
Alford, Robert, with Scoble, Harry M. *Bureaucracy and participation: Political cultures in four Wisconsin cities.* Chicago: Rand McNally, 1969.
Anderon, James G. *Bureaucracy in education.* Baltimore: Johns Hopkins Press, 1968.
Bachrach, Peter, & Baratz, Morton. *Power and poverty, theory and practice.* New York: Oxford University Press, 1970.
Bailey, Stephen K., & Mosher, Edith K. *ESEA: The office of education administers a law.* Syracuse, N.Y.: Syracuse University Press, 1968.
Citizen action in education. Boston, Mass.: Newsletter of the Institute for Responsive Education.
The community and the schools. *Harvard Educational Review,* 1972.
Cronin, Joseph M. The federal takeover: Should the junior partner run the firm? *Phi Delta Kappan,* April 1976, pp. 499-501.
Cushman, M. L. *The governance of teacher education.* Berkeley, Calif.: McCutchan Publishing Co., 1977.
Derthick, Martha. *The influence of federal grants.* Cambridge: Harvard University Press, 1970.
Donovan, John C. *The politics of poverty.* Indianapolis, Ind.: Pegasus, 1967.
Fainstein, Norman, & Fainstein, Susan S. Innovation in urban bureaucracies: Clients and change. *American Behavioral Scientist,* March-April 1972, *15,* 511-530.
Fantini, Mario D., Gittel, Marilyn, & Magat, Richard. *Community control and the urban school.* New York: Praeger, 1970.
Freeman, Tenton C. et al. Locating leaders in local communities: A comparison of some alternative approaches. *American Sociological Review,* October 1963, *28,* 791-798.
Gelhorn, Walter. *When Americans complain: Governmental grievance procedures.* Cambridge, Mass.: Harvard University Press, 1966.
Gelhorn, Walter. *Ombudsmen and others.* Cambridge, Mass.: Harvard University Press, 1967.
Gittell, Marilyn. *Participants and participation: A study of school policy in New York City.* New York: Praeger, 1967.
Gottlieb, Naomi. *The welfare bind.* New York: Columbia University Press, 1974.
Katz, M. From voluntarism to bureaucracy in American education. *Sociology of Education,* Summer 1971, *44,* 297-332.
Kershow, Joseph A. *Government against poverty.* Chicago: Markham, 1970.
Kimbrough, Ralph B. *Political power and educational decision-making.* Chicago: Rand McNally, 1964.
Kirst, Michael. The growth of federal influence in education. In *The uses of the sociology of education,* National Society for the Study of Education Yearbook. Chicago: University of Chicago Press, 1973. pp. 448-477.
Lazin, F. A. The failure of federal enforcement of civil rights regulations in public housing, 1963-1971: The co-optation of a federal agency by its local constituency. *Policy Sciences,* 1973, *14,* 263-273.
Lipset, Seymour M. Bureaucracy and social reform. *Research studies,* Washington State University, 1949, *17,* 11-17.
Litwak, Eugene, & Meyer, Henry J. Administrative styles and community linkages of public schools: Some theoretical considerations. Albert J. Reiss, Jr., (Ed.), *Schools in a changing society.* New York: The Free Press, 1965.
Marris, P., & Rein, M. *Dilemmas of social reform.* Atherton, 1967.
Murphy, J. T. Title I of ESEA: The politics of implementing educational reform. *Harvard Educational Review,* February 1971, *41,* 35-63.
Reagen, M. *The new federalism.* New York: Oxford University Press, 1972.
Rogers, David, et al. *New York City and the politics of school desegregation.* New York: Center for Urban Education, 1968.
Sarason, Seymour B., & Associates. *Human services and resources networks.* San Francisco: Joseph Bass, 1977.

Sproull, Lee, Weiner, Stephen, & Wolf, David. *Organization and anarchy: belief, bureaucracy, and politics in a new federal agency.* Unpublished manuscript, Stanford, Calif.: Stanford Graduate School of Education, July 1975.

Summerfield, Harry. *Power and process: The formulation and limits of federal educational policy.* Berkeley, Calif.: McCutchan, 1974.

Thomas, Robert D. Intergovernmental coordination in the implementation of national air and water pollution policies. In C. G. Jones & R. D. Thomas (Eds.), *Public policy making in a federal system.* Beverly Hills, Calif.: Sage Publications, 1976, pp. 39-62.

Turk, Herman. Interorganizational networks in urban society: Initial perspectives and comparative research. *American Sociological Review,* February 1970, *35,* 1-18.

Vosburgh, William W., & Hyman, Drew. Advocacy and bureaucracy: The life and times of a decentralized citizen's advocacy program. *Administrative Science Quarterly.*

Warren, Roland, et al. *The structure of urban reform: Community decision organizations in stability and change.* Indianapolis, Ind.: D. C. Heath, 1974.

Weber, Max. Bureaucracy. in H. H. Gerth & C. W. Mills (Eds.), *From Max Weber: Essays in sociology.* N.Y.: Galaxy Books, 1958, pp. 196-244.

Zeigler, Harman, et al. *Governing American schools: Political interaction in local school districts.* Belmont, Calif.: Duxbury Press, 1974.

School Governance and its Community Sociopolitical Environment

Laurence Iannaccone

We waste our time talking about community power structures if we are not talking about politics. Power structures exist to influence governmental decisions, which is what politics are about. Politics are about the management of conflicts over public issues, influenced by conflicting private interests, and within distinct battlefields of governmental arenas for decision making. To become more sensitive to the mutual dependence among schools, communities, and the nation, including the influences of different types of power structures on the schools, we need some acquaintance with the issues, interests, and constitutional arrangements of American educational politics.

SERVICE AND POLITICAL FUNCTIONS

Banfield and Wilson (1963) saw government as performing two general sorts of functions: a service function and a political function. The service function refers to those processes that will meet some perceived social need. In educational institutions the service function is much more singular than it is in local governmental units.

Many believe that the service function is the only function of educational institutions. Educators themselves have been among the prime perpetrators of this dying myth (Iannaccone, 1967). Few would challenge the statement that education in America is a governmental function, but some would argue that a governmental function can exist without politics. This paper rejects that position. School districts are governance structures which also have a political function. The political function of governmental institutions is to manage conflict, that is, to settle disputes between group and individual interests over issues of public importance. A conflict can arise out of disagreements over the values that an educational institution allocates (Cobb & Elder, 1972). This type of conflict is concerned with *what* gets allocated. For instance, there have been disputes over subject-centered versus pupil-centered approaches to educating children. Another example is the clothing allowance controversy in Massachusetts, where the parents of Title I children argued successfully that Title I monies could be used for clothing allowances (Hughes & Hughes, 1972).

Other conflicts have centered around the scarcity of the values that are allocated. In this case the issue is *who* gets what (Easton, 1965). For example, the distribution of "high-quality" teachers among black and white schools has been the center of controversy in some localities.

The service and political functions of government might not be distinguished as separate activities except for the fact that public controversy surrounds the latter function. A controversy, as conflict, may be thought of as a condition existing between two or more individuals or groups characterized by some overt sign of hostility between them (Aubert, 1963). The stakes are considered high; the outcomes are of central concern to the protagonists; the controversy is important; and strong emotions are involved. As a result, the application of expertise may not be sufficient to resolve such a dispute. At one time, educators were able to handle controversies by putting up the umbrella of expertise. However, although the umbrella still functions from time to time and from location to location, it is apparently becoming less adequate. In the governmental world, when traditional ways of operating are challenged and begin to break down, fundamental constitutional realities become more visible, and basic issues re-emerge at a new level of consciousness. These developments can be seen in educational governance today.

CONSTITUTIONAL REALITIES

The 1970's introduced an "Era of Enlightenment" in the politics of education. In the course of this decade the least understood and singularly important fact about public education will become popular knowledge: Every policy of any importance is determined at the state level. Because the Constitution of the United States makes no direct reference to education, it is a legal responsibility of the states. Yet for most people concerned about educational policy, the immediacy of the local system and the visibility of programs initiated at the federal level result in disproportionate efforts to influence policy at these levels rather than at the state level.

The American system of government is a federal system: Important powers and responsibilities are *shared* among levels of government. The system is one of a family of governments with shared responsibilities for conflict management rather than an hierarchical one in which conflict management is primarily allocated to the central, national-level government. In education, major policy areas are ultimately and decisively determined at the state level. Local school systems may raise funds, but they do so as agents of the state using procedures established by the state. Local systems may hire teachers, but the teachers must meet state standards. The length of the school year, the curriculum, provision of special education programs, introduction of accountability systems— all are state-level determinations. Even the decision to accept and spend federal aid for education programs is a state-level decision over which the federal government has no direct control. And the research on federal program implementation demonstrates that state educational politics largely detemine the outcome of federal policy (Berke & Kirst, 1972; Iannaccone, 1974).

A POLITICAL-IDEOLOGICAL ROLE

The federal government's role is nevertheless important in education. Instead of looking at its control functions, the political analyst might better pay attention to another function. Federal programs have begun to adjust the balance between poorer and richer districts and between urban and nonurban school districts as federal funds have been targeted toward areas of poverty (Berke & Kirst, 1972). More than the funds allocated, the federal government's role in articulating political symbols is significant. These symbols may be seen in White House statements, especially those made by the President. They appear in federal court decisions, particularly the ones handed down by the Supreme Court. Finally, the categorical grant may be seen as having a similar symbolic function even when the administration of categorical programs is partially blunted.

Federal political symbols of policy direction have an indirect but, in the long run, potent effect on the political beliefs of Americans, particularly in the areas of race and economic inequalities and in a growing awareness of the need to accept pluralism in educational services for different people. It is here, in the long-term influence on the political ideology of Americans about education for all Americans, that the political conflicts and decisions at the federal level are likely to have their greatest impact. This is historically the way in which the federal government has always had its most significant effect on education, from the Northwest Ordinance that preceded the Constitution, on to the present. Federal intervention has frequently enlarged the scope of education and lifted the sights of educators, often in spite of their initial opposition. For example, political forces at the state and local level long were dispassionate about the inadequacies of the education provided to the poor. Because of the nature of our political system however, the constellation of forces at the national level was dissatisfied and subsequently enacted Title I of the Elementary and Secondary Education Act (ESEA). Many educators, unable to move their local or state political systems to provide resources insuring greater opportunities for the poor, were pleased at this new opportunity to do so. As a matter of fact, some superintendents asked a political scientist working in the politics of desegregation for advice on how to get their districts under court order to desegregate! The federal actions provided legitimacy for them through political symbols.

CONSTITUTIONAL REALITY

The position of the state in educational policy development appears to have emerged from the confluence of two sets of attitudes, one set dealing primarily with educational governance and the other encompassing government in general.

The first set of attitudes may be referred to as the dual sovereignty thesis (Iannaccone & Cistone, 1974). The dual sovereignty thesis consists of two attitudes. One arises out of constitutional provisions. The United States Constitution makes no mention of education, but does grant the states responsibility for those areas that the federal government has not reserved for itself.

> Most state constitutions make local education a legal responsibility of the state. The United States Constitution is silent with regard to education; consequently, education is a reserved power of the states. These three levels of educational government interact on policies, but only state statutes stipulate in detail how schools are to be governed. (Wirt & Kirst, 1972, p. 111)

The other attitude producing a dual sovereignty pattern is the public's belief that education is a local responsibility. This attitude, the religion of localism, reflects the feeling of local districts that they "can only be protected by pursuing a policy of isolation and freedom from state control" (Wirt & Kirst, 1972, p. 131).

The confluence of these two attitudes has resulted in a state-local sharing of powers based on constitutional law and political tradition. The power of political myths widely held is illustrated in this tradition. Constitution and law notwithstanding, no school board can exercise its legal authority to change attendance-area boundaries without a political fight. During most of this century, states with undisputed constitutional power over school districts have faced the political reality of consolidation by using a form of births, extra funds, to unify districts. Balance between these forces has been maintained by the education profession.

> . . . the dual sovereignty produces dominant influence by organized schoolmen, which in turn functions to prevent the breakdown of the competing state and local governments. (Iannaccone & Cistone, 1974, p. 27)

The second set of attitudes influencing the position of the state in educational policy development deals with the relationship among the various levels of government. Reagon (1972) termed this relationship "federalism." Although a number of people have looked at federalism in a number of ways, one useful approach centers on the positions people take on the federal role vis-a-vis the local role in government. Those who favor the federal role look to the federal government as the means of establishing and maintaining uniform conditions throughout the country. Those who champion the local role may see the federal government as providing necessary support to local and state goals (Elazar, 1972). The interaction of these two orientations has resulted in a system of intergovernmental relations that represents a marble-cake pattern of sharing of governmental functions (Grodzins, 1966).

"To put the matter bluntly, government in the United States is chaotic!" exclaimed Grodzins (1963, p. 1). Perhaps "chaotic" is somewhat excessive; nevertheless, a dynamic interplay does persist between federal, state and local government. The intergovernmental affair in educational policy making can be best described as follows:

> The federal system is not accurately symbolized by a neat layer cake of three distinct and separate planes. A far more realistic symbol is that of the marble cake. Wherever you slice through it you reveal an inseparable mixture of different colored ingredients. There is not neat horizontal stratification. Vertical and diagonal lines almost obliterate the horizontal ones, and in some places there are unexpected whirls and an imperceptible merging of colors, so that it is difficult to tell where one ends and the other begins. So it is with federal, state, and local responsibilities in the chaotic marble cake of American government. (Grodzins, 1963, pp. 3-4)

A formal constitutional interpretation of educational governance sets clearly defined boundaries around the state as the "keystone" of American government and particularly of the governance of education. In practice, these constitutional boundaries are continually changing. Although they appear to be lawfully static, the dynamics of politics transcends them on an informal basis. Individuals and groups influence the state educational policy-making system, seeking changes in policies and constantly redefining the system's actual boundaries.

For our purposes, it is important to recognize that American education, within the federal system, is neither centralized nor decentralized: it is noncentralized. If we examine the education function of government as a political subsystem of the larger American political system, it is immediately apparent that distribution of governmental power is a result of complex relationships among the various levels of government in order to achieve common policy outcomes. Thus, a pattern of sharing responsibility for governance, rather than a hierarchy of governments, characterizes the relationships within the family of governments in America.

The education profession tended to dominate this intergovernmental structure until recently. The domination appears to have been strongest on the implementation/delivery-service end of the game. Is it surprising, then, that educators deny and often refuse to even look at the conflict-management or political aspect of it?

COMMUNITY INFLUENCES

A second governmental context of schools that deliver the service is the local school district's political community. The politics of the local education authority appear to be influenced by the larger state and national contexts, "macro-politics"; by the politics of schools at building and classroom levels, "micro-politics"; and by community influences. So McGivney and Moynihan (1972) argued that school districts respond to macropolitical pressures within a zone of tolerance, which, if exceeded, produces political conflict. The West Virginia and Boston cases of 1974-75 illustrate their points of excess. Title I programs, as modified at state and local levels, fall within that zone. The state and federal contexts have been discussed above. The micropolitics of education will be addressed later in this paper. Community influences will be briefly discussed here.

Research on school board social composition and community power structure abounds, but has given us little useful guidance for action. Few community power studies relate community power structure directly to education. These studies have generated more conflict among scholars than useful findings about the effects of community power structures on education. A major thesis of most of these studies is that the interlock, duplication, and overlapping of leadership roles (sometimes of behind-the-scenes, invisible power figures) serves to channel community policy into a few hands, resulting in community coordination. That picture of political life in education has weaknesses. First, it appears to reflect small rural districts most and urban districts least. Also, it appears to reflect conditions in the southeast, to be useful there and in smaller rural communities rather than elsewhere (Kimbrough, 1964). Elsewhere at least, it appears that school board elections increasingly reflect rapidly changing populations (Iannaccone, 1967) and register voter feelings that are broader than local educational politics and have little to do with local community power structures (Thorstead, 1974). Studies of northeastern, northwestern, and midwestern suburbs suggest that school decision making is a highly specialized area in which professional, expert, formal officeholders are decision makers most of the time, with episodic crises sometimes disturbing their routine operations (Bloomberg & Sunshine, 1963; Crain, 1968; Martin, 1962; Pellegrin, 1968; Rosenthal, 1969).

Within the constitutional and legal framework, the local school district may attempt to resolve conflicts over policy by applying general norms. The norms of school board members are central to the resolution of disputes at the local level. These norms may reflect community values. Crain (1968), in a study on school desegregation, presented data indicating that value orientations associated with certain demographic, community-type, and electoral characteristics, had a bearing on the degree of acquiescence to desegregation policy by selected school boards. Acquiescence was high in cities where a balance of power existed; in these cities, board members had high socioeconomic status, high cohesion, and a high degree of liberalism. For working-class cities, acquiescence was low, with low-to-medium cohesion and liberalism.

Minar (1966), exploring the links between the school system and its social environment, noted that communities of better-educated populations and people in professional or managerial occupations displayed less school board conflict. He attributed this to their larger supply of conflict-management skills and norms. Minar inferred that in high-status, low-conflict school districts, school board norms place a higher value on the technical authority of the superintendent, place less value on representativeness, and give the superintendent considerable latitude in decisions. Conversely, school board norms in low-status, high-conflict communities place a lower value on technical expertise, place more value on representativeness, and are less inclined to grant the superintendent latitude (Cistone & Hennessy, 1971).

The continuum of homogeneous to heterogeneous community characteristics appears to be one of the most, if not *the* most, powerful underlying factors explaining variability in degrees of political conflict faced by school districts. It is the source of the new politics of education translated into political "stress." Uncontained diversity increasing over time produces political conflict in educational governments. Diversity is a key concept to explain the growing stress and heightened political conflicts faced by schools today. Some attention to its sources seems worthwhile.

POLITICAL IMPACT OF CULTURAL PLURALISM

School board members, no less than administrators, teachers, and other members of the middle class, will experience difficulty understanding the fundamental roots of the conflict and stress produced by diversity of political cultures. So, distinguishing sociocultural diversity from political diversity is essential at the outset. By political diversity, I mean those sets of political demands (in Easton's terms) that are in conflict with each other about a governmental service, *but which also support the value of diversity in those services to accommodate different social subcultures* (Easton, 1953). That is, although cultural pluralism lies at the roots of political diversity, it is not the same, nor will political diversity automatically follow cultural differences. Cultural pluralism is a necessary but not sufficient condition for the creation of political-cultural demands reflecting—or representing—it in government. There are at least three other sociocultural factors in addition to cultural pluralism that tend to produce increased diversity of political demands and that can become governmentally disruptive, other things being equal. One is geographic mobility, resulting in defeat of incumbent school board members (Iannaccone, 1967; Iannaccone & Lutz, 1970; Iannaccone & Wiles, 1971). Another is social mobility brought about by affluence (increased socioeconomic status), with its increasing demands for different educational services (Iannaccone, 1972). Third, there is the changing demand on higher expectations produced by education itself, apart from geographic or social mobility (Iannaccone, 1972).

Given these conditions, it is not surprising that we have seen increased efforts from the macropolitical level, especially state and national, to influence both the educational services rendered and the governance system of education. Illustrations of this may be seen in federal legislation like Title I of ESEA; federal and state court decisions like Brown versus the Board of Education and Serrano versus Priest; and state legislation like that which reorganized New York City's educational government. Similarly, administrative regulations such as the United States Department of Health, Education and Welfare's recent demands to eliminate sexism in physical education, can be cited. However, macrogovernmental action and formal decisions—legislative, judicial, and administrative—are not the only tools for conflict resolution, and sometimes they are not the most important ones. Norms of the education profession provide another base for resolution of policy disputes.

PROFESSIONAL NORMS, A POLITICAL TOOL

Professions are extremely closed systems. To become a school superintendent, for example, commonly requires that an individual attend a school of education to obtain credentials for teaching. Next, that individual must teach for a number of years and take additional coursework in order to be certified for administration. Then, it is usual for an aspirant to the superintendent's position to serve as a principal. Finally, a stint on the central office staff may be required. After all this, the individual may become a superintendent (Carlson, 1972).

These socialization steps help to instill professional norms. One way in which these norms function is to sanctify the profession:

> Every profession seeks to surround its practitioners with elements of mystery with the imputation of specialized knowledge apart from that held by others... The cloak of the professional mystique helps protect both the professional's self image and his public relationships. (Iannaccone & Lutz, 1970, pp. 54-55)

Educational policy is rooted in professional sanctification. Historically, this connection grew out of the superintendent's central position as the architect of school board policy and the expeditor of its implementation. The strength of expertise as a molder of policy and carrier of values and preferred ways of thinking about education appears to be losing some ground. But it is still a powerful and "relatively more informed" technique for the development of policy. It is rooted in the micropolitical experience of teaching in the classroom. Any attempt to understand the educational organization's political realities must take the concept of professional autonomy as central to that understanding. The focal issue has always been—but even more so now as cultural pluralism and variations in local building attendance areas increasingly influence educational politics—the appropriate balance between the influence of professional expertise and the influence of representativeness in the decisions of educational organizations. The political-cultural mix most influential in a given community displays a basic orientation toward this balance.

Issues more fundamental than notions of power structure are: the political-cultural mix of a district, especially as it values expertise in contrast to representativeness; and the degree of heterogeneity or homogeneity in the district. The degree of metropolitanization or urbanization of a district appears to have implications for its political-cultural mix and is significant in predicting board and district political conflict (Minar, 1964; Zeigler & Jennings, 1974). So, the larger the district *and* the more heterogeneous the population, the more conflict it experiences. Similarly, the more the municipal-reform politics characterize the political culture of the local government generally, the greater is the respect for expertise and professional autonomy in education. Conversely, the more that traditional machine or precinct/ward politics characterize the government, the less is professional autonomy valued and the more is representativeness in government prized (Cistone, 1971). Even in the largest school districts—for example, those of New York, Chicago, Los Angeles, and Boston—the political mix that characterizes city politics influences the degree of conflict and respect for the value of professional autonomy experienced by the schools (Iannaccone, 1971). So, for example, although organized school employees are central political actors in the educational government of all cities, which employee organizations are dominant depends on the mix of political cultures in the particular city. In Boston, blue-collar workers are most influential; in New York City, top organizational political power is found in a coalition of teachers and administrators; however, Chicago balanced professional and blue-collar power through the Daley machine (Iannaccone, 1971). Thus, the particular political-cultural mix of a city, especially its beliefs about the values of professional expertise versus representativeness in government, influences that city's educational politics.

Minar (1964) noted that education is a separate local governmental operation; therefore, it produces a plural or separate community power structure. He suggested that a classification system is needed for education that compares technical expertise related to professional autonomy versus community power structure. The essential issue that he posed is whether groups external to the educational government, competing or complementary, actually seek to influence its decision processes. Thus, how highly professional expertise and autonomy are prized, and how much consensus on that value exists in a community, are more important issues for educational politics than is the nature of a community's general power structure. The professional political ideology of autonomy is rooted in the realities of the classroom teacher's task as controlled by the realities of organizational life in the classroom.

A MICROPOLITICAL FOCUS

It was no accident of Watergate or Vietnam, nor a chance weakness in the dominant parties producing the Democratic convention events of 1968 and the Republican incumbency of Gerald Ford, that might have made possible the combination of the radical conservatism of Ronald Reagan and the populism of George Wallace into a new national political party. A more fundamental dilemma lies at the heart of all these events. That dilemma is found in the failure of macro-American politics to give adequate expression to micropolitics—the day-to-day interests of citizens where they live and work. Macropolitical processes and governmental structures in education suffer from the same weakness.

The micropolitics of education are found in and around the school building. They are concerned with the interactions and political ideologies of social systems of teachers, administrators, and students within school buildings. They are also concerned with issues of interaction between professional and lay subsystems at the building level.

There are several reasons for the teacher to focus on the micropolitics of education: (a) this political arena is closest to his or her ongoing work; (b) building-level politics share the universal underlying issues of educational politics in our day; (c) building-level politics display the elements of the educational operation that come nearest to producing unique features in the politics of education; (d) finally, solving the political problems at the building level in education can make a major contribution to the fundamental governance dilemma faced by democratic societies.

One word of caution—if the teacher is too emotionally involved in the political aspects of a job and protects himself or herself from that emotional reaction by defining the job and the events he or she shares in an apolitical and purely educational way, whatever that may mean, then the proximity of events and the small size of the social systems the teacher shares will block his or her vision and learning. If instead, the teacher overcomes that block, he or she can see the political world differently, enhance his or her skill at operating in it, and enjoy it more.

The internal political world of the school building is comparatively tangible. For example, the social system's use of space in a building is often so clear that it can almost be touched. A social system's use of space in its work world structurally reflects the interrelationships of its components, its authority relationships, and its norms. Most faculties reflect their pattern of interaction in seating arrangements at faculty meetings, in differential use of teacher lounges—sometimes the boiler room is one—and especially in lunch cliques (Iannaccone, 1962). From another perspective, ideas of turf ownership—whose territorial responsibility and domain are certain parts of the building?—correspond to authority relationships in buildings. Usually, the principal "owns," and is responsible for, the corridors, cafeteria, and johns, in addition to his or her office. "My classroom" is the individual teacher's domain; "our lounge" may be one or more teacher groups' territory. Such statements reflect the authority system of principal, teacher, and student. They also indicate the norm of autonomy for the individual classroom teacher and selective collegial relations within the building outside the classroom—with some but not all teachers and certainly not the principal.

A PROFESSIONAL DILEMMA

The professional demand for autonomy is, from a political science view, a political ideology. The demand for autonomy is found in all professions and is related as much to the perception of expertise held by the professionals as it is to a demand for status. It is, in effect, a demand to be allowed to use one's expertise with minimum hindrance from others.

Seeing the professional demand for autonomy as an essential aspect of professional work, helps to clarify the meaning of that demand. Professional autonomy attempts to deal with a common professional dilemma, especially acute for the helping professions, in which securing the client's willing support and cooperation is a necessary though not sufficient condition for expertise to work. The professional engages in two sorts of activities, those necessary to get the job done most expertly and those needed to invoke client cooperation in the client's own development. The need to secure willing cooperation from the client produces a dilemma for the professional. He or she has a choice: to use authority, either legal or expert, to tell the client what to do, or to rest less on authority and rely more on eliciting cooperation by sharing decision making with the client. The dilemma is real, not merely ideological. It is rooted in the fact that the client must be psychologically engaged in his or her own growth. Moreover, much of what the client must do to use the expert guidance of the professional must be done by the client when the professional is not immediately observing him or her. The best prescription given by the professional to the client will do no good if the client fails to take it as prescribed.

THE DILEMMA COMPOUNDED IN EDUCATION

Four conditions in American education compound this fundamental, universal dilemma of the professional: the compulsory nature of the service and the consequent lack of choice as a safety valve; the setting in which the service is rendered; the mode of payment for the service; and the teacher's turf itself.

In some professions, the dilemma of authority versus shared decision making is partly resolved by the fact that professionals and their clients engage in a pattern of selection by which each, in effect, chooses the other. The fact that I choose a particular physician or lawyer to provide me with professional services already partly resolves the difficulty faced by them in getting me to follow their advice. Mutual choice is a safety valve. Where instead, the range of choices for selection is much more restricted for both practitioner and client, the dilemma between reliance on authority and shared decision making becomes even greater.

Compulsory education laws oblige the clients, both students and parents, to accept the service; at least, the students must be in the school. It is all well and good to say that if I reject medical services, that rejection may cost me my life, but the fact that I may reject the service produces a different psychological effect than does the absence of choice for students and parents. Operationally, compulsory education means that with rare exceptions, students must be in a particular school—in their attendance area—in a particular track and a certain classroom under a specific teacher with a given group of students.

The student's conditions of organizational membership are not theirs to determine. They have no organizationally legitimate autonomy at all! Their response to that is the only freedom they have. The law cannot and does not determine how students or their parents respond to that reality. Consequently, some degree of alienation usually characterizes the nature of the students' response. Alienation allows them to withhold some of their identity from compulsory membership in the organization. Not allowing themselves to be pushed around by authority figures and not allowing themselves to become psychologically engaged in the tasks set for them are ways of exercising the freedom of choice left.

Students vary greatly in the degree to which their response is one of alienation. But teachers confronted with the need to gain the cooperation of the client are faced with the problem of how to decrease the alienation. That problem in turn confronts them with the classic dilemma of whether to depend on legal authority or to develop shared decision-making patterns in the classroom. Without a significant degree of autonomy the teacher cannot make that choice. Operationally in fact, most teachers shuttle between the invocation of their authority and shared decision-making patterns. Thus, one source of the demand for teacher autonomy is the fact of compulsory education.

A second root of the demand for teacher autonomy is the nature of the organization within which the service is provided. The teacher's professional service is rendered within a complex and large-scale organization. Three implications of this fact increase the demand for teacher autonomy. First, the teacher, unlike many other professionals, is not solely responsible to the client and colleagues for his or her performance. He or she is also responsible to the school organization. Second, responsibility for the client's welfare is shared by the teacher with others, particularly the relatively nebulous "system." Most important, this professional cannot select clients. Students are by and large assigned to teachers by the system's relatively impersonal decision-making processes.

The events of the 1950's and 1960's decreased the range of choices available to teachers. Similarly, those events decreased the range of choices once available to clients. Defining the classroom as turf was therefore inevitable. Demanding autonomy over the activities on that turf was also inevitable.

A third element that compounds the dilemma of the teacher is the way in which the service is paid for—indirectly, by the larger society through its macropolitical decision-making structures. The point is not the fact that general government taxation pays for education. It is instead the fact that client choice has no direct relationship to the economic base of education. For example, a nationalized health system may also be tax based; however, so long as client choice influences the practitioner's income, some degree of economic bond links the client and the practitioner. That bond is missing in the teacher-student relationship.

Three major consequences flow from this fact. One is that the teacher-student relationship is weakened by the absence of an economic bond. However much professions deny the importance of the economic bond between them and the client, it normally exists. Indeed, the fact that professions loudly proclaim that the economic bond is not a major motivation for the professional should help us see that there are ethical bonds too, but does not permit us to deny the economic one.

A second consequence of the mode of payment used in public education is that it produces a different economic bond between the teacher and the larger society, a bond that often militates against client interests.

There are two distinct lay publics with an interest in education. One is the micro-lay-public—the public most concerned with the delivery of the service close to the teacher and student at the building level. The other is the macro-lay-public—the interest that is societal and general in nature.

The micro-lay-public is one of the roots, the external one, in the micro-politics of education. Its economic link to the building is extremely indirect and only meaningful as a source of influence when this public is aggregated and therefore submerged within the larger interest of the general society. The micro-lay-public has different needs and expresses some different values than the other public. It is concerned with different outcomes too. It is concerned specifically with the particular students and their peculiar needs. It is concerned with particular classrooms and teachers and their specific operations. It lacks governmental mechanisms for the expression of its values and interests in outcome because combining them for general board policy, for example, requires compromising their peculiar nature. Further, the political ideology of American educational government has usually systematically denied the importance of such "special interest."

On the other hand, the economic bond produced by the payment system of education maximizes the set of interests expressed by the other lay public. The structure of American government is designed to make the general public interest effective. The ideology of American educational government supports that interest. Is it therefore surprising to find that governmental bodies in education display an economic concern more often than any other single one?

School people have generally been responsive to the public interests that have the monopoly on the economic bond and good access to the governance mechanisms. The rise of militant teacher organizations is in part attributable to the need that teachers feel to compete effectively in that large arena of macropolitics. Teachers have a better chance of protecting their autonomy and turf from lay interests at the micropolitical level than from lay interests at the macrolevel.

A fourth element making autonomy an inevitable teacher demand arises from the conditions of the teacher's turf itself. Strong boundary maintenance and strong beliefs in the society about autonomy protect that territory externally. Internally, however, teaching of one sort or another goes on in a classroom. Schooling is not tutorial in nature; the teacher works with groups, the classroom group being the largest. Teacher autonomy and teacher authority in the classroom are intimately related. The teacher is confronted with some degree of student alienation. To maintain the social system of the room, the teacher must usually give way to some of the implications of that alienation. However, in order to produce significant task accomplishment, the teacher cannot surrender to it. So, the teacher dilemma is the professional one of shuttling between use of authority and the use of shared decision making. Realistically, most teachers combine some of each.

Teacher tactics are easier to develop if the turf is well bounded and the belief in autonomy is well established. Maintaining that condition involves two wars on two battlefields much of the time. Within the classroom the teacher must wrestle with the problem of student alienation, which, if attacked too directly, is likely to become hostility. At the same time, the teacher needs to keep parents and administrators off that battlefield to have the autonomy needed to balance the internal dilemma.

Teachers have long been ambivalent about administrative structures and roles. On the one hand, the stronger the boundary, the greater the teacher's autonomy; on the other hand, the principal's office, school board regulations, and the central office can help to protect the teacher's turf from intervention by the micro-lay-public. So, for example, a strong principal may mean that somewhat less autonomy exists for the classroom teacher vis-a-vis the administration. But strong administration provides greater protection against attempts by parents and community groups to influence the classroom. Also, a strong principal often helps teachers deal with the internal classroom needs for group maintenance and task accomplishment; teachers can be supported by appeals to the principal's authority.

For most of this century teachers have supported administrator-led organizations in the political realm. That support has provided them with economic benefits and increased autonomy against public interference. School administrators have been socialized as teachers and share the ideology of teacher autonomy. It is reinforced when they are called upon to support teachers. Thus, through socialization and job mobility the political ideology of the microlevel developed from the classroom need for autonomy, and reinforced at the building level, translates easily to the macropolitical ideology of the local education agency, state, and nation.

THE ADULT SOCIAL SYSTEM OF THE SCHOOL

Shifting our focus from the classroom to the adult social system at the building level, we find that the internal micropolitics of that unit are structured into informal groups with group values, processes, and outcomes. Such informal teacher groups produce an informal complex organization and are the basic elements of the internal micropolitics of the building. This is not to say that group formation is political in origin. All to the contrary, social needs are primary, but once the informal organization is in existence, it has the capacity to move toward political action. Hence, administrators frequently fear such groups even before they move in such a direction. That fear is a fundamental error of administrators. Primary groups will exist in any case. Attempts to suppress them will have the result of either increasing teacher alienation from administration or more often, making teachers become politically active. The development of teacher militancy in the last 20 years has been partly because administrators in large numbers made that error.

AN EXTERNAL PROBLEM TOO

Much of the evidence of the last 20 years also indicates a rising client demand for a more direct voice in the delivery of educational services. We should not be surprised if indirect representation—a sort of proxy political vote—fails to satisfy people. Also, community demands at the building level, particularly in the larger cities, are directed against the service as performed by the same professionals who would then be their representatives. Then, too, there are significant social-class differences, with associated differences in values, between education professionals and deprived neighborhoods.

One result of the major conflicts in the macropolitics of education has been to reduce the capacity of even internal building politics to reach and influence central office and board activities, until the internal politics erupt violently enough to force attention or engage broader segments of the body politic. Ironically, when broad sections of the school district's public are brought into the conflict, the embattled coalitions on both sides are likely to lose sight of the peculiar concerns of a particular building's interest.

There is no ultimate resolution of the tension between lay control and professional autonomy in educational government. Nor is it likely that many serious persons would want it to be all of either. The conflicts, therefore, have usually raged around the question of when is there too much of which.

A second basic, perennial, and equally pervasive issue is the tension between administrator or management control and teacher autonomy. The present governance system in education is to a large extent a product of the educational-and-municipal-reform movements of the turn of the century. School boards, particularly in urban districts, were reformed. Small boards replaced large boards, at-large board elections or appointments usually replaced precinct or ward elections, the political party often lost a large measure of influence over board members, and school board composition became more upper middle class.

On the positive side, these developments decreased party political patronage and corruption in education, and they appear to have increased economic efficiency in education. But the reform also decreased the representative nature of educational governance. They were elitist in their consequences. Americans appear to have believed that for a long time the gains outweighed the costs.

On a second front the reforms increased the professional standing of school administrators first and then that of teachers. Their de facto, if not de jure, autonomy and leadership increased vis-a-vis the board. Their training and credentials improved and increased. Teacher professionalism also improved markedly. So did the social recognition, income, and autonomy of teachers. Their autonomy was particularly increased against lay interference from both the board and building-level lay interests. But there were some costs. Administrator control of teachers appeared to have increased also. Certainly their control of the National Education Association and its state affiliates did. Further, the interaction of teacher and parents appeared to have become more selectively middle class. Clearly, the supportive relationship between the school and the family around their students/children declined. Again, for a long time the gains seemed to have outweighed the costs.

In small and rural districts these reforms had little or slow effect. The small and rural districts still displayed the dominance of lay control. However, that dominance was less rigorously used and less acutely felt because of the close ties of small communities and the homogeneity of the cultures that produced boards, administrators, teachers, students, and parents. In the large cities, by contrast, the reforms not only decreased public and professional interaction at the building level, but were also a major ideological victory for upper-middle-class values. The reforms denied the value of cultural pluralism—at least as found in the cities—and reflected a belief in the melting pot theory. Indeed, the schools were seen as having a major role in the melting pot process to eliminate the cultural pluralism resulting from immigration especially. Again, this elitist governmental development with its attendant single-class, monocultural values, seems to have worked for a time with certain urban groups. But in this way, too, by the denial of cultural pluralism—in fact, by attempt to eliminate it through education—the reformed educational governance system was less representative than it had been.

Two additional and apparently unanticipated consequences followed the immediate results of the reform developments. First, the United States experienced, at least until recently, a dramatic and continuing shift of populations out of rural and into metropolitan areas. This demographic shift was a factor in changing the fiscal base of education to increase the state's contributions and decrease district inequalities, often at the expense to some degree, of what once were the richer districts, the urban ones.

The second most consistent outcome of the educational governance system in the 20th century was the decline in the number of small school districts, especially single school units. In small school districts the general taxpayer interest and the interest of the micro-lay-public converge and may both be accommodated by one board. But overall, increasingly larger groups of citizens were being governed by fewer school districts. The small board was supposed to represent the interests of increasingly larger numbers of people. The effective political distance from school building to board became longer and longer in the process.

Thus, the initial push that the reforms gave to increasing professional autonomy at the expense of lay control was carried much further. The early increase of administrator dominance over teachers and their organizations was compounded, especially in the larger urban districts and in state lobbies. Surely, such a sequential drift over years could not continue endlessly. Some system disestablishment and disequilibrium were bound to take place eventually. The effects of such developments were felt in stress and strains, especially at the micropolitical level, which was virtually cut off from the macropolitical world, lacking governmental mechanisms for articulation and aggregation of microinterests.

TWO PUBLIC INTERESTS

The educational governance system provides representation, mechanisms of access, and ideological legitimacy for the expressions and influence of the general interest of the larger society. It does not do so for lay interests at the building level. Worse, it ignores those units in its representative structures. The structural bias of local board elections becomes almost comical when, for example, as in Los Angeles in the late 1960's, Chicano parents and interest groups found easier access to state assembly representatives than to school board members. Urban dwellers have sometimes found it easier to influence legislation than school board policy. The political processes of the present local district force lay groups at the building level to merge or aggregate their demands with other buildings to produce a common policy, ignoring cultural pluralism and individual needs of students at the same time. The political ideology of boards is slowly changing, but it still reflects many of the upper-middle-class, municipal-reform beliefs that are hostile toward cultural pluralism. Thus, structural, process, and ideological factors facilitate the political efficacy of a social class and a macropolitics of lay general-interest groups. The same factors repress the emergence of an effective micropolitics of lay groups at building levels.

In sum, the educational governance system of this country has never in this century developed appropriate structure, ideology, or processes for the effective articulation and aggregation of micro-, school-building politics—for either teachers or client interest groups. The internal structure of teacher organizations may pay attention to this problem partly through internal representation and grievance systems. The lay interests at the building level appear never to have been adequately represented by the lay interests at the macropolitical level, except in the smallest school governments. As teachers appear to gain in the struggle for power against administrators and board, the client interest best found in the micropolitics of the building may be even more likely to be lost in the shuffle of power.

The most significant political outcomes of the last 20 years of increasing conflict in education may yet be found in the micropolitics of lay interest groups. If the long-range effects of the readjustments of power among teacher organizations, administrators, and boards close the boundaries of policy making further against that micro-lay-interest, either of two results can be predicted. The clients, students and parents, will become more alienated and refuse even more often to support the schools. Alternately, they will be energized into near-explosive political action to restructure educational governance, so as to have an impact on the issues that concern them at the delivery end of the structure. More probable for the next era in the politics of education is a combination of both. In any case, although the roots of much of the politics of education are to be found in micropolitical systems, their effects must be translated through the macrosystems to influence the future of educational governance.

We need to know more about how to link the demographic bases of a district's political cultures to the governance of schools. We have, in fact, never had such representation except in the single-school-building district. To readjust the balance of influence between teachers and administrators alone is not enough. To balance a community elite off against a professional elite is not adequate. As Bachrach (1967) said:

> The crucial issue of democracy is not the composition of the elite—for the man on the bottom it makes little difference whether the command emanates from an elite of the rich and the wellborn or from an elite of workers and farmers. Instead the issue is whether democracy can diffuse power sufficiently throughout society to inculcate among people of all walks of life a justifiable feeling that they have the power to participate in decisions which affect themselves and the common life of the community, especially the immediate community in which they work and spend most of their waking hours and energy. (p. 92)

Historically, school politics have played a role in creating an educated citizenry. There really is only one way to teach responsibility; that is to give people responsibility, let them make decisions, and let them experience the consequences of their choices. Operating with this belief may not be the American dream, but it was the American faith. Without it, the American dream will become a nightmare. Given the experiences of Watergate and Vietnam, how much worse can the mistakes of the common person be than those of the brightest and best? The start of America's third century appears to be a good time to renew that faith.

REFERENCES

Aubert, V. Competition and dissemus: Two types of conflict and of conflict resolution. *Journal of Conflict Resolution,* March 1963, *5,* 26-43.
Bachrach, P. *The theory of democratic elitism.* Toronto, Canada: Little, Brown, 1967.
Banfield, E. C., & Wilson, J. Q. *City politics.* Cambridge, Mass.: Harvard University Press, 1963.
Berke, J. S., & Kirst, M. W. *Federal aid to education.* Lexington, Mass.: D. C. Heath, 1972.
Bloomberg, W., Jr., & Sunshine, M. *Suburban power structures and public education.* Syracuse, N.Y.: Syracuse University Press, 1963.
Carlson, R. O. *School superintendents: Careers and performance.* Columbus, Ohio: Merrill, 1972.
Cistone, P. J. Municipal political structure and role allocation in educational decision-making: An exploration of one linkage. *Urban Education,* 1971, *6,* 147-165.
Cistone, P. J., & Hennessy, B. School board members' attitudes and administrative norms: An exploration of public-regardingness. *Midwest Journal of Political Science,* 1971, *15,* 587-594.
Cobb, R. W., & Elder, C. D. *Participation in American politics.* Boston: Allyn and Bacon, 1972.
Crain, R. L. *The politics of school desegregation.* Chicago: Aldine, 1968.
Easton, D. *The political system.* New York: Knopf, 1953.
Easton, D. *A framework for political analysis.* Englewood Cliffs, N.J.: Prentice-Hall, 1965.
Elazar, D. Fiscal questions and political answers in intergovernmental finance. *Public Administration Review,* 1972, *32,* 471-478.

Grodzins, M. Centralization and decentralization in the American federal system. In R. Goldwin (Ed.), *A nation of states: Essays on the American federal system.* Chicago: Rand McNally, 1963.

Grodzins, M. *The American system.* Chicago: Rand McNally, 1966.

Hughes, J. F., & Hughes, A. O. *Equal education: A new national perspective.* Bloomington: University of Indiana Press, 1972.

Iannaccone, L. The informal organization. In D. E. Griffiths, D. Clark, R. Wynn, & L. Iannaccone (Eds.), *Organizing schools for effective education.* Danville, Ill.: Interstate, 1962. Pp. 225-296.

Iannaccone, L. *Politics in education.* New York: Center for Applied Research in Education, 1967.

Iannaccone, L. *Problems of financing inner city schools.* Columbus: Ohio State University Research Foundation, 1971.

Iannaccone, L. School district policy development in the sobering seventies. In N. Robinson & A. H. Elliot (Eds.), *The politics of education: Current issues.* Burnaby, British Columbia: Simon Fraser University, 1972. Pp. 15-29.

Iannaccone, L. State education departments: Their role in administering federal programs. *New York University Education Quarterly,* 1974, *5*(2), 13-17.

Iannaccone, L., & Cistone, P. J. *The politics of education.* Eugene: University of Oregon, 1974.

Iannaccone, L., & Lutz, F. W. *Politics, power, and policy.* Columbus, Ohio: Merrill, 1970.

Iannaccone, L., & Wiles, D. K. The changing politics of urban education. *Education and Urban Society,* 1971, *3,* 255-264.

Kimbrough, R. B. *Political power and educational decision-making.* Chicago: Rand McNally, 1964.

Martin, R. C. *Government and the suburban school.* Syracuse, N.Y.: Syracuse University Press, 1962.

McGivney, J. H., & Moynihan, W. School and community. *Teachers College Record,* 1972, *74,* 317-356.

Minar, D. W. Community characteristics, conflict, and power structures. In R. S. Cahill and S. P. Hencley (Eds.), *The politics of education in the local community.* Danville, Ill.: Interstate, 1964. Pp. 125-143.

Pellegrin, R. J. *An analysis of sources and processes of innovation in education.* Eugene: University of Oregon, Center for the Advanced Study of Educational Administration, 1968.

Reagon, M. *The new federalism.* New York: Oxford University Press, 1972.

Rosenthal, A. *Pedagogues and power: Teacher groups in school politics.* Syracuse, N.Y.: Syracuse University Press, 1969.

Thorstead, R. R. Predicting school board member defeat: Demographic and political variables that influence school board elections. Unpublished doctoral dissertation, University of California, Riverside, 1974.

Wirt, F. M., & Kirst, M. W. *The political web of American schools.* Boston: Little, Brown, 1972.

Zeigler, H. L., & Jennings, K. *Governing American schools.* North Scituate, Mass.: Duxbury Press, 1974.

Government's Responsibility in Improving Education Outcomes

William L. Smith*

I would like to discuss the past role of the Office of Education, how we see the federal role of government in education, what the major problems are that we are attempting to address, and specific areas relating directly to what I call the revolutions in American education, which have implications not only for children, but for all of us adults.

USOE MISSIONS

The United States Office of Education (USOE) was established by Congress in 1876. Its basic purpose is stated as promoting the cause of education throughout the country. This original mission is still the base on which the Office of Education functions, even though new responsibilities are called for today to meet new demands.

If we were to sum up three basic missions that have been installed in USOE since 1876, the first is to provide rational leadership in the search for more effective education; the second, to continuously assess the state of education, and keep the country informed of what it is about, and what its needs are; and third, to administer legislation enacted by Congress, and entrusted to USOE. USOE is an instrument of Congress which provides legislation it is responsible for administering. USOE's leadership role is a function of its power to persuade and help those at state and local levels to effect change and improvement through rules, regulations, program policy, and technical assistance.

Although federal programs and ways of achieving them have changed, the three basic purposes mentioned above are consistent with USOE's function. The real question then becomes, "If this is our role, what then is the role of an educator in the Office of Education, or in what is usually called the federal bureaucracy?" It is a question of asking what needs to be done, how our responsibility can be effectively and efficiently carried out, and what the time lines are for achieving it.

Principal among issues that confront us today as "feds" are the continued efforts to define educational commitments, to conceptualize necessary actions to meet these commitments, and finally to implement

---

This article appeared in The Journal of Teacher Education, *Vol. 26, No. 1, Spring, 1975. pp 35-40.*

them. In many instances we failed to alleviate the problems toward which programs were aimed because we either entered the arena with limited understanding and capabilities, or failed to design the kind of program and implementation strategies that Congress had asked for.

With this in mind federal officials today are providing developmental and technical assistance to local projects which are stimulating change through research, information, dissemination, and capacity building at the local level.

FINANCING EDUCATION

Economics and the whole question of financing of education will become even more critical in the years ahead as education becomes an even larger component of the public budget. A brief look over the last few years indicates dramatic changes in the role of education. In 1958 when Sputnik was launched by the Russians, Congress passed the National Defense Education Act (NDEA). This was the first time that the citizenry had required Congress to provide resources to boost educational programming. In 1965, the Elementary and Secondary Education Act was passed, and this was the first time that the federal government became involved financially in a major part of educational programming. The Educational Amendments of 1972 was the third most significant money bill designed to involve the federal government in education.

Interestingly enough, during 1969 and 1970, secondary and elementary schools alone expended about 39.5 billion dollars. During 1973 and 1974, the same elementary and secondary schools expended some 56 billion dollars. During 1976 and 1977, those schools expended 82 billion dollars. In all of those years, approximately eight percent of public school revenue was derived from the federal government, 38 percent from state sources, 42 percent from local sources (mostly from property taxes), and 12 percent from other sources.

With the property taxes being the most regressive of any major tax, it becomes clear that improved ways of providing for public school revenue must be found. The differences among states regarding the extent to which they provide resources are astronomical. In Delaware, for example, 71 percent of state resources go to education. In New York, it is 44 percent, in New Hampshire, 10 percent.

When you look at the total budget in elementary, secondary, and post-secondary education in 1972 and 1973, you find a startling revelation. The budget was approximately 85 billion dollars in 1972. Of that 85 billion, 85 percent was locked into personnel salaries, benefits and fixed costs. In 1973, the budget was about 93 billion dollars. Of the 93 billion, again, 85 percent of the resources were locked into personnel and fixed costs. In 1976 and 1977 the total expenditure was 131 billion dollars. This suggests that you must consider eliminating funds eaten up by personnel, and do something about the personnel responsible for delivering educational services to children.

The existing division of authority within the education division and other federal agencies concerned with educational problems, involves questions of strategy that go beyond the considerations of overall federal roles. Consequently the focus of this presentation is on the federal role of education without major restrictions to specific Office of Education responsibility. The Education Amendments of 1972, 1974 and 1976 split many of the functions that had belonged in 1865 to the Office of Education and to other agencies within what we now call the Division of Education. The Assistant Secretary of Education now coordinates the Office of Education and the National Institute of Education (NIE) which is the research arm for nearly all of education. The Assistant Secretary has administrative responsibility for the Fund for the Improvement of Post-Secondary Education (FIPSE) which encourages innovative programs at the postsecondary level, and for the National Center for Education Statistics (NCES).

Of course the Department of Labor and many other agencies are also responsible for manpower training and the like.

FEDERAL RESPONSIBILITY IN EDUCATION

Several general criteria are proposed for helping us define when there is and is not an appropriate federal responsibility in American education. All of these criteria are subject to one general constraint. In the absence of special circumstances, the support and conduct of education is primarily a nonfederal responsibility. In elementary and secondary education, the general provision of educational service is largely a state and local responsibility. In postsecondary education, there is a broader basis for federal involvement and support, but there too, the basic responsibilities are state, local, and private.

In American society, we do not have the kind of centralized ministry of education system present in most foreign countries. Instead we have a highly decentralized state, local, and public system, and there seems to be no serious political force in American society which would fundamentally alter that present division of responsibility. Therefore, it will continue to be a decentralized program, the primary responsibility of state and local governments.

Thus, whenever any proposed federal education initiative or program is considered, we must first ask what the special and compelling circumstances are which make it a federal rather than state or local or individual task. With that fundamental consideration in mind, let me describe several basic criteria for determining federal responsibility.

1. It is necessary to address needs and problems which are national in scope and consequence. Although the bulk of routine educational tasks and responsibilities are the province of state, local, and private organizations, there are some educational needs and problems which transcend both the responsibility and/or capacity of state and local government. These are areas in which the social

and economic health of the nation or the fundamental rights of individuals are at stake, or where the activities and presence of the federal government itself generate specific federal responsibility.

Several examples illustrate these types of specific educational responsibilities. Within the context of addressing needs and problems that are national in scope, the existence of a group of children who do not have equal educational opportunity has increasingly been recognized. Local schools have been unable to give adequate education to a significant portion of the population. The economically poor, the handicapped, and children from non-English speaking families are prime targets.

Serious society-wide consequences flow from their lack of adequate education—lower productivity, higher unemployment, increased welfare burdens, and a general inability of those individuals to lead satisfying lives, much less carry out their responsibilities as citizens.

As a nation, what we have said in effect is that the greatly increased difficulty in educating these children exceeds both the capacity and resources of local school systems. Because the consequences of their being inadequately educated are both serious and national in scope, the federal government should provide various forms of compensatory educational assistance and help state and local school systems meet their general educational responsibilities.

2. Federal involvement in compensatory education in order to establish real equality of education at elementary and secondary school levels is paralleled in postsecondary education.

3. In addition to the problems of compensatory education at the elementary, secondary and postsecondary levels, there exists throughout society a significant number of functionally illiterate adults, prey to all problems of dependency, lower productivity, and the like.

4. Elimination of segregated school systems appropriately requires federal involvement, both in legal enforcement through Title IV and programmatic assistance through the Emergency School Assistance Program. Similarly, the eradication of sexual, linguistic, age, and other forms of discrimination demands federal intervention. Title IX is a case in point.

5. The need to assure that the critical personnel shortage does not have crippling effects on the nation's economy and the functioning of its basic institutions will occasion federal support of personnel training in teaching, medicine, foreign affairs, and other areas.

6. Increased educational burdens as well as loss of resources and revenues resulting from the presence of federal installations and personnel clearly obligates the government to provide appropriate compensation when those federal facilities reduce the number of tax dollars going into a particular jurisdiction.

In terms of addressing needs and problems which are national in scope and consequence, we see that there is a definite federal role as it relates to those six items discussed above.

A second area of federal responsibility is advancing the state of the art of the quality and relevance of American education. It would make little sense to have all 50 states carrying out separate and redundant educational research programs. Thus, to develop new knowledge and more effective educational practices is uniquely an appropriate federal role.

SEVEN EDUCATIONAL PROBLEMS

The first and probably most important problem we have is the poor, i.e., the persistence of an economically, culturally, educationally disadvantaged, low-performing, poverty-bound group. This comprises about 20 percent of our total population. This problem should be our overriding priority, and one to which we should devote the bulk of our resources and creative energies.

The second major problem is the question of major cities. We are beginning to see that the educational dysfunctionality in the major cities may be so severe that it cannot be solved by remedies targeted on specific groups of students or on a simple equalization process.

The third major educational problem is the business of education and work and the fact that our young people do not see any relationship between what they receive in the classroom and the world of work.

The fourth major problem is quality of educational practices. The major educational problem we face is in mounting a productive research and development program and the development of extensive, useful research-based knowledge about the educational process and the effectiveness of methods and techniques. We all know the need, but the great problem we have faced is how is it orchestrated?

The fifth major problem is the growing inability of teachers to identify children with learning and/or behavioral problems in the regular classroom; to diagnose the level and degree of those problems; and to prescribe teaching and learning activities to meet the needs of these children. Add to this phenomenon the impact of Public Law 94-142 which requires the inclusion of handicapped children in the regular education program. Teachers, already frustrated by their inadequacy to cope with the affective responses of some children and youth, find their training obsolete to deal with the special educational needs of handicapped children assigned to them. This shows the quality of teacher education.

The sixth major problem is a question of educational management. We are beginning to recognize that there is an enormous difficulty on the part of those who have been educational managers today to meet the needs of different populations.

Finally, there is the question of resource allocation and equalization. It has to do with the question of the difference both between and among states with regard to the number of dollars spent on children.

Those are basic areas where the federal government has a role.

EIGHT REVOLUTIONS
1. The Teacher Revolution

There are a number of revolutions that have occurred which have implications for education. First is the teacher revolution. In 1955 I was a beginning teacher. I remember when the superintendent of schools informed me of what my future looked like. He said, "Smith, you may rest assured that in 36 years, you will reach your maximum." It took 36 years to make top dollar as a teacher in 1955 in Cleveland, Ohio.

I am sure there are some who never reached their maximum, even though they stayed 36 years. Remember those days? From 1964 on, the teacher revolution began. Teacher power became a way of life. Ironically, many superintendents of schools and school boards responsible for negotiating in those early days negotiated away more power than they had ever dreamed, simply because they didn't understand that teacher negotiation was here to stay.

So you must understand that the federal government, regardless of agency, and state and local governments too, will not negotiate programs without also negotiating with the teacher organization or union.

The real question becomes one of how we combine for those teachers the kind of responsibility that transcends the question of whether or not they are getting benefits and salary increases with whether or not they are getting better working conditions. How can we capitalize on this teacher education revolution in such a way that children will benefit more than they are now?

2. The Cultural Revolution

The second is probably the most startling revolution. I call it the cultural revolution. I break it into two parts—first, the minorities and the poor. The riots and burnings in Watts (1965), Detroit (1967), and Washington (1968) demonstrated the destructive nature of these big cities and made a tremendous impact upon education. It was one of the things accompanying the teacher revolution which allowed for the negotiating of a shorter time period to reach a maximum—a better retirement system to give teachers an opportunity to get out of the system earlier.

I submit the cultural revolution, especially in the big cities, had the same devastating effect in that we lost an awful lot of very talented teachers who could not deal with the question of cultural pluralism, cultural minorities asking to be included where they had been excluded.

On the other side of that coin, the cultural revolution, is the youth counterculture. I am sure you remember the number of universities where young people said, "No, we ain't going to take it no more like we used to." They got into major discussions about the value structure, about the relevance of what their school was offering.

I am reminded of a document in the *Harvard Educational Review* which discussed the state of value constructs today as they move from traditional to emergent values, specifically about the traditional value system as being a part of the Puritan ethic, that time and work were important. The emergent value system was one where one discussed neither the future nor the past. One talked about the present and its utilitarian value.

Our youth counterculture moved dramatically to show that they were no longer interested in need gratification that was long term, nor in the tradition and history of the past. They were interested in what we were doing today.

3. The Knowledge Revolution

The third revolution is the knowledge revolution. This is split into two parts as well. The first is data acquisition.

How does one manage data? How does one sort out and discriminate in the use of information? We have had to go to computers, systems analysis and retrieval systems, for we found that the classroom teacher could no longer stand in front of the class and be the dispenser of all this information, because it was coming to children faster in some instances than it was coming to the teacher.

Television and technology are the second half of the knowledge revolution. They no longer allowed children to use their imagination as books and the radio had done. So it became difficult for the classroom teacher to stand in front of children as we historically had done.

Today, there are more people in the classroom. There are paraprofessionals, volunteer parents, and the teacher, and then there are the televisions that monitor what teachers are doing through microteaching. Thus we move away from the dispenser of information to the facilitator of the learning process, simply because the volume of information is too great for any one person to be the sole custodian. What we have to move toward is the process of acquiring information that meets the needs of children, regardless of where they are.

Of course, the advent of technology, whether it happened to be television, computers, or a series of other things, was part of the basis for the competency-based teacher education movement, which began to talk about something that we had not talked about before: the measurement of performance, both for teachers and students. It was something that we were not accustomed to and a lot of us said, "We ain't buying it."

The reason we weren't buying it was simply because it was not the way we were taught. It had no meaning for us. It did not provide an opportunity to talk about past and future in a way that makes sense. This is critical, because we are a technological age, a postindustrial age, that is going to be performance-oriented whether we like it or not.

4. Collaboration Revolution

The fourth revolution is what I call the participatory-democracy collaboration revolution, which had grown out of the need for publicizing what we were saying we are going to do.

We are going to have to deal with the question of collaboration in a way that we have not ever dreamed before, because collaboration means a readjustment of power. So many of us who have power don't want to give it up. There are all kinds of power. When we talk about collaboration, we now are talking about how we are going to have to share that power differently.

In the context of the waste of resources, collaboration becomes most critical. A university is no longer going to be able to sit back and say that they have the ivory tower that will allow them to sit and contemplate what is going to happen to children. For in the new power relationship, the necessary dollars will not necessarily be at that institution, and that institution is going to have to deliver services it had not delivered before.

5. The Financial Crisis

The fifth revolution is the financial crisis. In elementary, secondary, and postsecondary education, there are today major financial crises. They have a tremendous effect upon the education of children. If you look at big cities like Philadelphia and Detroit, you recognize that they are operating with deficit spending. There has to be special legislation provided to allow them to advance.

There is also a financial crisis in postsecondary education. One of the things that this administration is moving toward is the reduction of institutional support and more movement of resources to the individual. This does not clearly help institutions of higher learning, because the institutional support is elsewhere. But those financial crises affect the education of children.

6. Court Litigation

The sixth revolution is court litigation. There are at least 15 to 19 states today that have right-to-education litigation. There are another 10 or 12 that have already declared, through either state legislature mandating or state educational agency administration, that children must have the right to education and that the institution has a responsibility for the teaching and learning process for all children.

The *Lau vs. Nichols* case in San Francisco clearly has implications for bicultural children, because it says that now school systems are responsible for providing educational opportunity in both languages. Think of the impact of the right to education and the *Lau-Nichols* decision on a population that already has 85 percent of its budget locked into personnel. We have personnel who are not in a position to deal with children who have handicaps or who are bilingual and bicultural.

7. The Legislative Revolution

The seventh revolution is the legislative revolution. State legislatures are mandating, whether they have a data base or not, for new educational opportunities. They are talking about accountability in ways that they have not yet defined, except that they see the need for it. The unfortunate thing about competency-based teacher education is that it talks about systematic management and responsibility and public disclosure of objectives. The legislature has said that is accountability. Many states have legislated 50 million dollars for competency-based teacher education, and then asked, "What is it?"

8. Role Ambiguity

The last revolution is the constant ambiguity of roles. What is it that the school is responsible for? I found an article by Peter Brooks, who had spent a year in France on an exchange program. He said:

> In France, school is resolutely school. The affective problems of socialization, the ideals of citizenship, the definitions of self in society, do not fall within the school's purview. No doubt, partly as a consequence, the level of anxiety associated with the problems of education in America is infinitely lower in France. Education in America has come to appear more and more the institutional expression of national anxiety. The schools stand at a tension-laden frontier between the ideal and the actual, responsible both for the indoctrination in one and training in the other.
>
> The pervasive democratic demand for a citizenry enlightened and enabled to participate in the affairs of the public through an education that both prepares them for life and raises their sight to life's values has placed a tremendous burden of responsibility on the school, one that has probably grown intolerable as the gap between ideal and real has become more apparent. The myth of homogeneous values and goals is more and more radically put to question. Paradoxically and dangerously, as the society has become less and less sure of its consensus and direction, it has asked the schools to do more and more both in mastering reality and in merely relating it (pp.4-5).

Brooks goes on to point out that education has been overburdened by the weight of aspiration, confronted with the force of an unmastered reality, and is close to collapse through anxiety. He argues, and I would agree, that we must stop and ask the question, "Should the schools be the focal point of all that we call social change?"

What *does* lie within the school's power to perform? How can it perform? Will it perform? Brooks argues that the beginning of the solution to the problems of schools may have to start with their partial withdrawal from the social battlefield. He is arguing that we no longer can expect the school, as a social institution, to be responsible for filling voids that other social institutions have not maintained.

The fact that we have the luxury of compulsory attendance for children, allowing for a captive audience, should not be the basis for asking the schools to do more than they are able to do, more than teachers are trained to do, more than administrators are trained to do. If we do not understand that the question of alternatives has to be viewed on a continuum, then we may be already on the road to disaster.

We now find that there are advocates for deschooling, and advocates who say that the schools cannot change themselves. There are those who say that given an opportunity, the schools could, in fact, change if they were able to define what it is they are trained for and have the capacity to do.

We argue that there is a continuum called "continuity to change." We are going to have to recognize that there are things in the tradition, whether transmission of the cultural heritage or simply value constructs from the adult community, that are foundations for what is occurring.

We talk about the continuity of what *is*. Yet what we have got to think about is the fact that what Chautauqua probably does better than any other institution is to provide for perennial learning. Who is to say now that young children should end their education when they finish high school or graduate from college? If perennial learning does not become the way of our entire society, then we are never going to move to an open learning system but will keep a closed teaching system.

REFERENCES

Andrews, Theodore. *Atlanta or Atlantis?* Albany: New York State Education Department, Multi-State Consortium on Performance-Based Teacher Education, 1974.

Brooks, Peter. Toward a critical reading of reality. Sequence 4. Paper prepared for Project OPEN, Southampton (N.Y.) Summer Sequences 1974, pursuant to a grant from the US administered through TTT. Copies available from the author at Yale University.

Houston, W. Robert & Howsam, Robert B. (Eds.). *Competency-based teacher education: Progress, problems, and prospects.* Palo Alto: Science Research Associates, 1972.

Lau vs. Nichols 414 U.S. 563 (1974).

Rosner, Benjamin. *The power of competency-based teacher education.* Report of the Committee on National Program Priorities in Teacher Education. Boston: Allyn & Bacon, 1972.

Part II
Schools, Communities, and Teachers in Action

Part I of this book is a series of readings about the social environment of schools. The purpose of this section is to help teachers and other students of organizations to: first, explore issues raised in the preceding section; second, test and apply concepts introduced in this and the previous two volumes; and third, further examine the characteristics of and underlying assumptions about organizations that individuals and/or schools encounter daily.

Part II contains a wide array of activities for student and teacher use. The instructor should select activities in the order that best suits the instructional purpose and participant levels of awareness. Participants or instructors may want to modify or add to the list of activities offered.

SUMMARY OF ACTIVITIES

1. The Choate County Textbook Controversy: Cultures in Clash. A school system with its social environment is explored in this case study which is based upon a factual incident.
2. *Conrack.* In this film a teacher encounters a community culturally different from his own.
3. Alternate Concepts of Power and Leadership. This article encourages readers to discuss the role of teachers and teacher organizations in taking responsibility for schools.
4. Ethnomethodology. This series of exercises shows techniques for exposing and examining common assumptions that guide behavior.

Activity 1
The Choate County Textbook Controversy: Cultures In Clash

A CASE STUDY

The intent of this case study is to present a problem situation in which schools and the community are in conflict. Having studied the readings in the preceding section of this volume, participants will now examine characteristics of schools and communities as organizations to understand better how schools function in the social environment.

This case, selected for discussion purposes, is but one example that instructors might use. Other prepared cases, or cases written by students and instructors are also rich resources for study. The analysis of the Choate County case represents one interpretation of a complex set of factors and series of events. Participants are encouraged to develop their own interpretations which are, of course, equally valid.

Suggestions for Use of Case

The Choate County textbook controversy is a lengthy and complex case which leads participants to engage in extensive discussions. The case should be read thoroughly before participants are brought together to examine the concepts it highlights. Throughout the discussions, participants should relate the events in the case to their readings in Part I and to materials contained in Volumes I and II of this series. In discussions, participants will explore these and other concepts:

- Bureaucracy
- Hierarchy
- Values/value conflict
- Power
- Authority
- Influence
- Professionalism
- Particularism
- Rights and obligations
- Leadership
- Status
- Standardized procedures
- Autonomy
- Boundary maintenance
- Norms/norm conflict
- Roles/role conflict
- Conflict resolution

After a thorough reading of the case participants should:

- Review the case and identify key characters, groups, and organizations
- Review the list of concepts above, and briefly define the terms drawing examples from the case. Other concepts should be added as they are identified by the participants.
- Identify and summarize the problem or problems that the case illustrates. List the problems so the group can refer to them during the discussion.
- Analyze the case. Attempt to answer questions such as:
  — What events led to the problem?
  — What alternative action strategies might various groups have taken? What outcomes might have resulted?

- What are the critical issues that the case illustrates? What are critical turning points where the problems are alleviated or intensified?
- How does the study of organizations contribute to an understanding of the case?
• Relate the case to the readings. Ask participants to identify major points made by the authors in Part I and to locate illustrations of those points in the case.
• Conclude the case. Summarize the key concepts which participants have discussed and refer them to the author's analysis of the case which is contained in Activity 1. End with a reaction to the author's analysis.

THE CHOATE COUNTY TEXTBOOK CONTROVERSY: CULTURES IN CLASH

Part A: The Setting

The Choate County school system is one of the largest school districts in the nation. Serving 51,000 students, it encompasses an area of 850 square miles. The district is situated in the heart of Appalachia, where the population is distinctly white, Anglo-Saxon, and protestant. Less than one percent of the citizens is nonwhite and only three percent are first or second generation foreign-born. Nevertheless, the county includes extremely diverse cultural groups. It is heavily industrialized, with a majority of workers employed in coal mining and chemical and glass manufacturing plants, but many workers are drawn from surrounding small towns and rural areas. Forty percent of the county's population is rural, nonfarm. (Less than one percent live on farms.) Most of the Choate County schools are small and scattered throughout remote, rural areas of the country. The remainder of the population is equally divided between central city and suburban communities.

The county form of school district, and the geographical and cultural diversity within it, are central to an understanding of the textbook controversy that arose in Choate County: how it developed, what occurred, how it was resolved, and what its implications have been for education in the county, and for education everywhere.

Part B: Background

The area encompasses the state's capital and most sophisticated city as well as many isolated rural communities known as "hollows." The contrasts between urban and rural life are pronounced and pervasive. Like the rest of the state, some regions of the county are relatively desolate and wild, with settlements that were once coal camps located near the coal mines. Other urban-suburban areas, found along the river valley, are highly industrialized. The commercial and industrial center of the state dominates this region.

The modern world has intruded into the hollows in recent years but the traditional values and fundamentalist religions, long dominant there, flourish with undiminished fervor. The children from the hollows have been drawn into an increasingly urban and liberal school system as their small schools in outlying areas have been closed down and then merged into a consolidated system. Consolidation has transformed the schoolhouse from a cornerstone of the community to an element of a large bureaucracy dominated by professional expertise and middle-class values. In many cases, schools are miles from home, teachers are anonymous, and parents do not participate in any of the schools' activities. As in other parts of the country this loss of parental control and involvement in education has led to increasing criticism of schools. Parents' views are not sought and seldom are considered. The "good" education their children receive in the urbanized schools seems a far cry from the traditional education parents value.

Without a catalyst this uneasy situation might still exist. But in the spring of 1974 the Choate County school board made a decision about textbooks which brought the parents out of the hollows in outraged fury and permanently into the decision-making councils of the Choate County school system. To understand what happened, it is necessary to review some events leading up to the summer of 1974.

In 1965 eleven community representatives were appointed to the school district's curriculum council. The council was formed as an advisory group to the board of education regarding the direction of desired curriculum changes. All the members of the council, professionals and lay persons, were appointed. The lay people did not represent a cross section of the county population. There were no fundamentalist ministers, coal miners or undereducated rural people selected who might reflect the values of the Appalachian folk culture. On the whole the citizens selected were well educated, middle or upper-middle class and community leaders.

The curriculum council typically dealt with relatively mundane matters and there was little or no disagreement with professional option or recommendations. But in the spring of 1973 for the first time lay members of the council were openly opposed to a curriculum program supported by the school administration. Subsequently, for various reasons, the committee was reorganized and was to have been replaced by two new committees, one consisting of professionals and one composed of lay persons.

However, teachers and administrators reacted with apathy, and insufficient applications were received to initiate this new system. As a result, neither committee was formally organized until the 1975-76 school year. The demise of the original curriculum council, disbanded prior to the 1973-74 school year, left the county school system (and school board) without any other organized vehicle for community input. The National Education Association's Inquiry Report stated that:

Not only did the school system fail to inform or consult with parent groups in advance of the textbook adoption, in early 1974, but it eliminated the one group—the Curriculum Advisory Council—through which there could be some degree of parental involvement. As noted earlier, the superintendent stated that this was done with the intent of establishing a more effective method of consultation with parents. But whatever the reason, the timing was unfortunate since it could appear to a distrustful public that the Council was dissolved as a means of concealing from the community the contemplated textbook adoptions.

It should be noted, however, that state codes require that all elementary basal textbooks be selected from the state board of education's multiple textbook list, and that the textbook selection committees, making their recommendations to the board of education at the county level, be composed *solely* of professional educators. Lay citizens may not be a part of the committee that recommends textbooks for adoption by the county board of education. Indeed, state law provides no mechanism for citizen participation on this topic.

The county's textbook selection committee consisted of five teachers. The board of education decided to adopt their recommendations for a set of basic and supplementary books to be used in the county's new federally subsidized English Language Arts program. With the provisions of federal guidelines, the books were selected to represent the full range of views and styles found in our society. Among the authors represented who were to provoke much of the controversy were Langston Hughes, James Baldwin, e.e. cummings, Dick Gregory, and Eldridge Cleaver.

Five years before the English Language Arts Program was devised, Choate County was divided by an issue which presaged the events of 1974. In April 1969, the board of education adopted a pilot program for sex education to be introduced into several of the county's schools. The program was killed largely through the efforts of a board member named Carrie Scott who had been elected on a platform opposing sex education. In 1974 Carrie Scott turned her efforts to banning books with the same conviction and organizational skills she had used so successfully five years earlier. The people who had supported her in her earlier fight, many of whom were from the rural, conservative communities, had tasted their first victory over a power structure which had always been remote and impervious to their views. They were with Ms. Scott in force when she took on the English Language Arts Program. Fueled by distrust of urban society, they now could launch an attack on a target close to home.

Part C: A Chronology of Events

In 1974 a seemingly routine selection of textbooks exploded into an intense and violent controversy. Ms. Carrie Scott accused the educational system of promulgating atheism and secular humanism by teaching situational ethics and by eliminating prayer and Bible reading from the school program. As a fundamentalist and board member, Ms. Scott asserted that infringement of her belief in a literal interpretation of the Bible as God's infallible word was as much a violation of religious neutrality as prayer in school. The chronology of events which follows provides some understanding of what happened.

Early 1974	The curriculum council which provided advisory citizen involvement in Choate County's textbook selection process was dissolved; the group intended to replace it was never organized.
March 12	Textbook selection committee submitted its list of book recommendations for the English Language Arts Program. The books were exhibited in the local library and the offices of the board of education. Little or no effort was made to encourage the public to review the books, and few people did.
May 16	The textbook selection committee presented its case in support of the books to the board of education.
May 16-June 27	Carrie Scott, a board member, campaigned against the book selections, attending church and community meetings, familiarizing the people most likely to oppose the books with the sections they were most likely to find offensive. Circulated with the excerpted materials were petitions demanding that use of the books be forbidden in the schools. The county school system waged no counter campaign in support of the books. Public opposition to the books was expressed by 27 ministers of fundamentalist churches. The Executive Board of the City Council of Parents and Teachers condemned those books they had read. Candidates for the state legislature and county government offices were lobbied by the anti-textbook groups. The State Human Relations Commission and the vice-president of the state NAACP expressed their support for use of the books.
June 27	The board of education voted 3-2 to purchase all the recommended materials except eight supplemental texts. Petitions containing 12,000 signatures were submitted to the board forbidding use in the schools of materials which "demean, foster skepticism, or foster disbelief" in such institutions as the family, the supernatural being, the free enterprise system, private property, the study of English grammar, and a vision of America as "one of the noblest civilizations that has existed." Ten ministers representing the more formally established religious denominations in the county expressed full support for the English Language Arts Program and the texts chosen to implement it in a petition submitted to the board.
Summer 1974	Antagonism to the textbooks widened as excerpted highlights were broadly publicized and local opposition groups formed.

Sept. 3	Schools opened but were picketed and boycotted by citizen groups. The dimensions of the split became clear for the first time. During the first two weeks of school pickets appeared at businesses, factories, and coal mines.
Sept. 4	3,500 coal miners engaged in wildcat strikes in support of the boycott.
Sept. 7	The first citizens group in support of the book selections was formed, the Choate County Coalition for Quality Education.
Sept. 10	The protesters succeeded in forcing the state capital's bus system to stop running.
Sept. 11	The board of education voted to withdraw the controversial books until they had been reviewed by a new 18-member citizens' textbook review committee chosen by the board members and the member elect (elected in May; due to take office in January) who would serve as chairman. This compromise was accepted initially by the protesters.
Sept. 12-16	Choate County schools were closed and all extracurricular activities cancelled as violent protests spread through the county. Gunfire hit school buses, firebombs were thrown at the cars of families trying to keep their children in the schools, schools were vandalized and some bombed, threatening phone calls were received by parents of children who had been attending schools. The state police were called in.
Sept. 24	Members of the citizens' textbook review committee were named.
Oct. 9	Six members of the citizens' textbook review committee who opposed the books, and an alternate, dropped off to form a rump review committee which subsequently issued a report rejecting 184 of the 254 titles they reviewed.
	The president of the board of education submitted his resignation two and one-half months before the end of his term in the hope of "cooling the controversy" and was replaced by the member elect.
Oct. 11	The superintendent of schools announced that he was job hunting.
Oct. 15	The citizens' textbook review committee recommended adoption of all the basic texts and supplemental texts with the provision that no student could be required to use books offensive to his or her religious beliefs or those of his or her parents. Some supplemental books remained to be reviewed.
Oct. 30	The county board of education building was dynamited and partially destroyed.
Nov. 8	The board of education voted 4-1 to accept most of the books for use in the schools although some were to be

made available only through the library and only to those students whose parents did not object to the contents. Alternative books were to be provided for the other students. Another motion was adopted prohibiting teachers from indoctrinating students with moral values or religious beliefs contrary to those of the students or their parents. These concessions were viewed as fair and reasonable by people in favor of the English Language Arts Program. The protests in the community continued unabated despite the compromise.

Nov. 16 The superintendent of schools and three board members were arrested and charged (along with the fourth probooks member who was out of town) with "contributing to the delinquency of minors by permitting un-American and un-Christian textbooks."
At the time of their arrests they were meeting with anti-book protest leaders and a minister who had agreed to mediate the dispute. They were released on bond after a court appearance.

Nov. 21 The board of education gave tentative approval to an extremely restrictive set of new guidelines for the future selection of textbooks which supporters of the English Language Arts Program thought could cripple the free learning process in the Choate County schools for years to come, if it were strictly implemented. Future textbook selections were to contain no material challenging the sanctity of the home, the teaching of traditional English grammar, loyalty to country or religious beliefs. Teachers were forbidden to make inquiries for discussion purposes into students' beliefs or behavior. Teachers were forbidden to teach "seditious" material, including anything that implied the superiority of a form of government other than our own. Textbooks must not contain any profanity or promote racial hatred.
The board agreed tentatively to accept a new process of textbook selection which would be dominated by parents (75%) with the power not only to advise but to censor which books would and would not be used.

Nov. 27 Several mayors from towns in the area proposed a plan for seceding from the county school districts, which was unworkable due to an inadequate tax base.

Dec. 12 The Choate County coalition for quality education urged that the board reject the new guidelines and procedures for textbook selection. These were later declared illegal by the state superintendent of schools.
The board adopted both the guidelines and the procedures at a meeting which was marred by physical assaults on the superintendent, the assistant superintendent and two board members. Racial epithets were shouted.

Part D: The Aftermath

Relative peace returned to Choate County's education system in the winter of 1975, but the education system was not, and perhaps never will be the same. Both sides profess to be dissatisfied with the solutions reached. Parents who objected to the use of the English Language Arts Program charge that their children feel they are disapproved of and at a disadvantage because they do not use the forbidden books and that books restricted to the library are actually in use in some classrooms. Parents who supported the book selections note that not all the books promised are available to those who want to use them and that restricting the use of some to the library has rendered them valueless. Teachers and principals have also complained of the complicated problems of implementing the board's decisions.

Interestingly, results from a newspaper poll done by questioning a random sampling of parents showed that while 70% of the parents of elementary school children refused permission to use those books restricted to the library, 75% of parents at the secondary level granted permission for use of all the books in the English Language Arts Program.

Education in Choate County has been affected in many other less measurable ways. The atmosphere in which teachers do their job has been drastically altered by the controversy. As a leader of a local teachers' group put it: "Teachers are afraid to use materials. They will not serve on textbooks committees. They mistrust the central office staff, the board of education, and the community. They are afraid for their safety, their peace of mind, and even for their jobs." And their fears do not appear to be unfounded. Carrie Scott has vowed, for instance, that as long as she remains on the board of education, no member of the textbook selection committee responsible for the English language arts book choices will ever serve on another faculty committee in Choate County.

The state legislature, feeling the aftershocks from the explosions in Choate County has been giving serious consideration to proposals amending the state school code to require that lay citizen members have places on state and county textbook selection committees and expanding state control over textbook selections to include both secondary and elementary levels.

A number of private christian schools have been organized and were enrolling almost two thousand students by the beginning of the 1975 school year.

During the evolution of the book fight, national organizations and individuals served to sustain the controversy by providing funds and legal assistance for antitextbooks groups as well as by keeping the controversy alive in the national media. Outside extremist groups converged on Choate County to provide rhetorical and organizational support as well as funding for the antibook campaign. Groups ranging from the John Birch Society and the Ku Klux Klan to the left-wing Socialist International Workers Party injected themselves into the conflict in the fall of 1974. How significant their impact was or how long lasting their influence in the community will be, cannot be known, but the distortions, innuendoes, and untruths they spread fired up an already dangerously inflammatory situation.

In the name of restoring decency to education in Choate County the 1974 protests prevented virtually any education at all for the children of the county for the three months when less than half of the children were in school. Besides missing part of a year's school work, some students whose parents opposed the language arts textbooks, were placed in a position of conflict between their parents' values and the values of other students and teachers. Many of those students who attended school throughout the protest often did so in an atmosphere of fear and tension. Many schools were divided by the controversy and students within these schools were segregated into groups of who could and who could not use the controversial texts.

Part E: Subsequent Events

When schools opened in 1976 in Choate County it was in an atmosphere of apprehensive quiet. People seemed more concerned about the quality of education than they had been before the controversy but were more cautious about expressing opposition to specific policies for fear of precipitating another explosion. The school system has become more sensitive to the views of parents and generally efforts are being made to be more accommodating to parents.

In 1975, the social studies program book selections were the first texts to be reviewed under the new guidelines. The lay screening committee, made up largely of parents, rejected a number of texts before sending an expurgated list to the professional textbook selection committee. Charging that the parent screening committee was sending "a mandate, not a choice," the Choate County coalition for quality education petitioned to the state superintendent of schools who ruled that the screening process violated state law. Parent screening groups can make recommendations, which are not binding, but they may not remove a book from consideration by the teacher selection committee.

In October, 1976, several events occurred which indicate how much the climate has changed in Choate County since the book controversy subsided.

- When a fundamentalist minister convicted in 1974 for conspiracy to dynamite the schools was sentenced to prison for three years after losing his final appeal on October 15, a minister from a large Episcopal church who had been a leader and spokesman for the probooks faction argued for leniency in his behalf saying that the offense had been a special circumstance which would not happen again.
- A rural minister announced that he had found obscene literature in use in the schools, arousing fears that the textbook controversy would be renewed. Instead his protest was routed through

the challenge procedure instituted by the schools, giving recourse to people with protests so that matters can be handled fairly and potentially explosive situations defused.
- Carrie Scott, the antibooks board member who keeps a vigilant eye on the schools for potential issues, sent a letter to parents urging that no children be allowed to be seen by school guidance counsellors because they espouse "value clarification." There has been no discernible drop in the number of children seeing counsellors and the issue does not appear to have aroused much interest in the community, raising the possibility that Ms. Scott may have discredited herself somewhat with her constituency or at least may have misjudged its present mood.
- A pollster commissioned to find out whether there was too much residual anger in the school system to risk putting a school construction bond issue on the November ballot urged the school board to go ahead with the bond issue. Bond issues have been generally supported in the past and pollster's findings did not indicate that there would be unusual and substantial opposition to a bond issue this year.

People do not talk much in Choate County today about the school books controversy and when they do talk about it, it is to people they know well. Support for the objectives of the book protesters is expressed by a wide cross-section of the community; opposition to the methods of protest is just as widespread. People live in fear of another explosion like the one in 1974 and for many, the less they talk or think about what happened, the more quickly it will go away.

AN ANALYSIS OF THE CHOATE COUNTY TEXTBOOK CONTROVERSY

Ronald G. Corwin
Roy A. Edelfelt

This case demonstrates the control role that bureaucracies occupy in modern societies. It also underscores the dilemmas involved in attempting to mesh a public service organization and its underlying ethic of professionalism with the principles of democracy.

In view of the violence perpetrated by the protest groups it is perhaps difficult to sympathize with their cause, and we do not condone all of their actions by any means. However, it seems impossible to fully comprehend the impact organizations have on the lives of citizens without considering the situation of the protesters.

They were actors in a larger, community-wide political struggle that was eventually played out within the school system. Such conflicts are inherent to modern organizations, because organizations are part of a larger society. The events in the case also demonstrate that public organizations are poorly equipped to handle unresolved *political* issues.

In any social system that harbors conflicting interests and values accommodations must be worked out among opposing groups. In our society, these compromises normally take place within the political system. But if conflicts are not worked out at that level their resolution is left to the public employees responsible for implementing policy. This cannot be an effective solution because bureaucracies are organized around the principles of efficiency and uniform treatment rather than around the democratic principles of dissent and accommodation of minority views. Thus, the Choate County school system was forced to assume weighty political responsibilities for which it was ill prepared.

Before attempting to assess the meaning and significance of the conflict, we shall approach the case by considering three linkage points in the school system where different principles must be accommodated:

1. The *school board,* which must adjust the demands of its constituency to the requirements of bureaucratic administration;
2. The school system *administration,* which must balance the need for standardization with the realities of existing diversity, and blend professional principles with administrative requirements;
3. The *teachers,* who must weigh the desirability of individual attention (particularism) against the risk of favoritism and treating some students unequally or unfairly.

The School Board

The school board, according to state law, is composed of five members elected by the voters of the county without reference to political party affiliation. No more than two members may be elected from any one of the seven magisterial districts within the county. Election to the school board is for six-year staggered terms of office. State law makes no provision for recall of members once they are seated. Elections take place during the May primary but successful candidates are not seated until the following January. Candidates are elected by a plurality; those with the most votes are winners even though they may have received no more than 10 to 20 percent of the total vote. Generally the rural population of the county has been under-represented on the school board. Indeed, the country-wide organization of school systems in the state has helped to create urban-rural conflicts. For many of the people who live outside the city limits, there is a sense of powerlessness born of the absence of an adequate voice to influence the decision-making process.

The school board operated under several constraints which should be kept in mind. First, like other school boards in this country, it was politically insulated, and not part of the larger political system. As a result, the protesters did not have the option of expressing their views through representatives on the local, state and national legislative bodies. Their opportunity to influence school policy was limited to a restricted access to a few board members, and the board remained unaware of the seriousness of citizen complaints.

Second, it seems unlikely that the few members of the school board could have adequately reflected the existing range and intensity of opinions in this county. And, since the board's constituencies disagreed among themselves, it did not have a clear public mandate to follow a particular course of action. This left the individual members with a great deal of discretion to act on the basis of their personal inclinations.

Third, the school board members were clearly on the side of legal authority in this clash between legal and traditional forms of authority. The protestors based their claims on the *traditional* right of families to control the way their children are socialized. The board members were responding to the *legal* obligation of school districts to provide for this socialization function. They were clearly inclined to take a legalistic and cosmopolitan view rather than defend the traditional, purely parochial values of their constituents. If this board is typical of the vast majority of school boards in the country, its members are more urbane, better educated, and more mobile than the majority of people in this country. In addition, board members sometimes use their positions as stepping stones to local and state political offices; the position orients them to the groups already in power. Several of these sentiments are reflected in this board in several ways: the Language Arts Program conformed to federal guidelines; the materials reflected a variety of life styles; and the board chose to solicit the assistance and advice of several state level organizations.

Fourth, the protestors' one advocate on the board chose to challenge rather than work the problem through the procedures of the system. Her power had a dual source: her position on the board combined with her popular outside base of support. She was able to challenge the legitimacy of the textbook selection process by mobilizing her personal, charismatic authority. Most organizations harbor such informal leaders who remain dormant but ready to seize opportunities as they arise in crises. The rise and fall of these contending leaders is an important source of organizational conflict and change.

The Administration

The full import of the protestor's marginal relationship with the board cannot be fully appreciated without considering the administration's position. The school board is legally responsible to the community but it can be co-opted by the school system and used to defend the administration's policies. This is because bureaucracies maintain profound inequities of power, a power which is concentrated in the hands of a few administrators who control resources and have access to information. These individuals are well insulated from the public and from their subordinates by the hierarchy, status deference, schedules and appointment calendars, secretaries and office doors. Thus, although in principle the school board exercises the ultimate authority over school policy, in practice the responsibility and much of the power is usually delegated to school administrators who have more time, information and resources, thus forcing the board to rely upon their judgments heavily.

The administration is charged with the difficult (if not impossible) task of giving efficient and equitable treatment to all members of the community. It therefore relies on standardized procedures such as rules, uniform materials and customary teaching practices. The case illustrates the use of the traditional managerial approach of professional educators from the superintendent down. It also demonstrates that it is not possible to standardize the treatment of such a diverse clientele without serious problems. No provisions were made for adjusting standards to accommodate the existing diversity. There was no option open to those parents who chose not to conform to the dominant values. It is not even clear that such options could have been provided without compromising the efficiency and equitability of the system. The one possibility that was mentioned, that of including concerned citizens on the Textbook Selection Committee, was ruled out. This left the textbook selection almost entirely in the hands of the professionals.

The county administration failed to take seriously the objections to the language arts materials. Professional judgment was considered sufficient to counter public attacks on the nature of the curriculum. Considering the multicultural, multiethnic nature of the language arts textbooks and the philosophy of the Textbook Selection Committee it would have been wise to gain a broad base of community support prior to the presentation of the list for adoption. The NEA report concluded that, "A vital preliminary part of the adoption procedure should have been wide dissemination of the true nature and objectives of the proposed materials in order to ward off in advance the half-truths of extremist attack." The election campaign platform of board member, Carrie Scott, should have given the administrative staff forewarning of the potential for an emotional, intense protest over the multicultural, multiethnic language arts materials in 1974. They also should have been aware of the lingering resentment felt by rural citizens over school consolidation.

The fundamental reason for their insensitivity, we believe, was that they were too well insulated from the public by bureaucratic structure and by their commitment to professional values of the teachers.

The Teachers

Just as the board backed up the administration, so the administration supported the teachers' autonomy. The administration was, in fact, forced to share its enormous power with the teachers, because they had several kinds of leverage:
- Because of the slippage of the hierarchy the teachers were in a position to interpret and selectively implement (and resist) administrative policies, thus forcing administrators to take their view into account;
- Administrators had to rely upon the teachers' experience and expertise; and
- Collectively, teachers could demand some voice in curriculum decisions.

Clearly, then, there was a convergence of power blocks within the school system—the board, the administration, and the teachers. They were able to defend the organization's autonomy by mutually reinforcing each other's position. It is extremely difficult for citizens to penetrate such a boundary system. Consequently, the teachers had a wide discretion. Their ability to decide which policies to enforce can be witnessed in this case. For example, it was noted that the guidelines finally adopted were not applied uniformly; some children experienced disapproval for not using the textbooks; some restricted books were actually used in the classrooms; and some promised books were made unavailable.

Conceivably, the teachers could have played a different role and acted as a safety valve in this situation, *if* they had initially been more sympathetic with the protestors' concerns and tried to take their values more fully into account. Most teachers, after all, subscribe to the principle of treating students as individuals and respecting their families' opinions. Some teachers in direct contact with students and their parents on a daily basis, are in a good position to understand the parent views and to mediate conflicting bureaucratic and community pressures.

However, the teachers were also operating under several constraints, including administrative expectations, their own subordinate position in the hierarchy, the federal guidelines, time pressures and reluctance to show favoritism, the clear threat the protestors posed to their autonomy, and the opposition of their professional association to these protest groups.

In addition to these factors, the teachers' ability and inclination to act on behalf of the parents was minimized by two dynamics within the conflict process itself. First, the teachers' discretion was narrowed as curriculum decisions became more centralized in response to external pressures on the system. The protestors focused their activities on the school board and on the administration; and more important perhaps, in the aftermath, the state department of education and the state legislature were playing more active roles. Because of the local board's political insulation, it was necessary to achieve political resolution at higher levels in the system. But it is indeed ironic that the educational system now seems likely to become even more standardized, over a larger area of the entire state, as a result of this local attack on standardization.

Second, this external threat to the system temporarily produced a united front against the community. The crisis forced teachers to choose between the school system and the parents, and their loyalties were clearly with the former, even though they might have felt freer to oppose the administration under other circumstances.

This left the protestors with no representation in the school system, as well as with little hope that the school board would seriously consider their views. Their fate hinged on the professional judgments of the teachers, and there was little prospect the teachers would be sympathetic. For, like the board members, they had cosmopolitan backgrounds shaped by their educational experience, their professional values, their regional and national associations, and their career mobility aspirations. Nor could the protestors be assured that the teachers would not use this authority to advance their own interests or to enhance their own personal status, and they had no acceptable way to assess the validity of the teachers' technical judgments about the effects of the materials. Understandably then, the protestors felt compelled to undertake the surveillance of the school on their own behalf, since they could not rely on anyone else to represent their views.

The teachers wanted to be sure that the materials reflected the range of cultural and ethnic diversity in the U.S. For this purpose they insisted on retaining final and exclusive authority to make curriculum decisions. This assumes that the lay citizens were less neutral and less qualified than they to make these judgments. But the parents were questioning the validity of the objective of teaching cultural diversity, not the teachers' technical qualifications for meeting it. Here, then, we can see how a profession's drive for academic freedom, and the authority and autonomy it represents, can clash with the values of some citizens seeking to protect their way of life. Teachers and parents were separated by sincere differences of opinion about what would best serve the interests of the students. And what is important is that they were both trying to control the destiny of others, i.e., the children. When two sides are so resolutely convinced of the righteousness of their own positions, there is no lasting resolution short of a political one. This brings us to a consideration of the underlying meaning of this conflict.

The Meaning of the Conflict

In a sense, this was a struggle over words. But it was much more than that. The textbooks were symbolic of much larger issues of value and power. It was a contest to control the young, and ultimately it led to a clash between two ways of life: local traditional values versus legal, cosmopolitan, modern ones. The protestors objected to the profanity and hedonism portrayed in some of the books, but more fundamentally they detested the *neutral* way in which their orthodox religion was treated and the fact that alternate life styles were presented as equally valid. Although value neutrality lays a foundation for the tolerance needed to hold a diverse, secular society together, it also can be taken as a means of depreciating sacred beliefs. Because the foundation of their beliefs was at stake, the conflict rapidly spread and became pervasive. It was no longer possible to treat the incident as a routine dispute over a particular issue.

Here then, is a people defending a traditional but still vibrant way of life against heavy odds. Though deplorable, the violence must be understood as something more than an exhibition of moral decay. It was a defense of community values that demonstrates the vitality of this way of life and the convictions of its defenders.

Since, as individuals, the protestors were no match for the sprawling organizations they were dealing with, they necessarily organized themselves into groups, and eventually into loose-knit, temporary coalitions. This process was facilitated by the relative homogeneity of their religious backgrounds, occupations and education. It is significant that the church leadership, a backbone of traditional societies, spearheaded the protest against another organization: a secular bureaucratized socialization agency. This process illustrates how organizations are used as weapons in conflict and thus how a society becomes progressively more differentiated as organizations form in response to conflict.

The protestors were being defensive, but they were not merely blindly, irrationally lashing out in general frustration against a loss of status. Their violence occurred in recognition of a basic fact: They had little hope of realizing their objectives *within* the professional bureaucracy, which had been unresponsive and seemingly unsympathetic to their views. As we have said, the school system, after all, was attempting to apply a highly standardized program to this diverse population with little provision for adjustments to large pockets of people to whom the standards seemed poorly adapted. The parents were expected to have faith in teachers whose decisions they did not fully understand or agree with. They were not represented on the original textbook selection committee, and they learned that they could have no legal authority on such committees anyway. The school board composition did not reflect the *intensity* of their feelings, their considerable numbers in this community, or their new-found organizational strength.

With little hope for exerting influence within the school system's formal channels, they chose to go outside, first with petitions, then with the politics of protest, and eventually with violence. And, once the authority system had been repudiated, there were few constraints left. The protest leaders' authority was only temporary and not well defined nor institutionalized. They did not and probably could not control the membership: violence ensued.

Thus, we end where we began. We see the cost of depoliticizing education. Political insulation can protect schools from partisan conflicts, but then this leaves few effective ways to resolve the political issues that do arise, before they erupt into rancorous conflict. Without formal outlets, without institutionalized means to resolve issues as they arise, minor issues are allowed to accumulate until they erupt into major outbreaks. Given differences of opinion, conflict is inherent in organizations, but the conflict can take different forms: (a) occasional but rancorous and uncontrolled outbreaks, which repudiate the legitimacy of the systems; or (b) continuous but routinized disputes within the system. The *form* that conflict takes may be the only choice that a multicultural society can make.

This case demonstrated, however, that the conflict process contains its own correctives. As a result of the conflict, the system has changed. The teachers have retained their authority, but the system has become more sensitive to parent groups. As a result of their surveillance, the protestors have forced into existence a set of checks and balances over professionals, and the protestors have moderated their demands.

A variety of formal and informal conflict resolution mechanisms have been put into place. Some of the passion has been channeled into private schools. The provision for citizen representation and review committees has been institutionalized, and a challenge procedure has been implemented. Thus, it can be clearly seen that organizational goals and procedures are not dictated solely, or even primarily, by criteria of administrative rationality. They evolve by conflict and compromise.

In closing, it is well to remember that democracy is based upon a fundamental irony: the majority can maintain its right to rule only if there is a chance that any dissenting minority, no matter how extreme its views, can be heard. Today's majority was itself once a minority, and there must be similar hope for all minorities. This is not to condone violence, but on the contrary, it is to observe that the school system, with its underlying ethic of professionalism, can thwart the opportunity of minorities to express their dissent and thus inadvertently *contribute* to a violent response. At the same time, with the proper organizational structure, school systems may be the only hope that minorities can be heard in our modern society.

Activity 2
Conrack*

A FILM

Conrack is a feature-length film that can be used to help participants explore the influence of the social environment on a remote school in South Carolina. The story is a moving one and participants may want to view the film, then discuss its impact on them and its literary merits and limitations before proceeding to an objective analysis. An objective analysis may include consideration of the following concepts:

- Bureaucracy
- Hierarchy
- Authority
- Co-optation
- Emulation
- Leadership
- Roles/role conflict
- Norms/norm conflict
- Values
- Slippage

The instructor may want to consider the following strategies for use of the film:

- Distribute discussion questions that can guide participants as they view the film. Some suggestions are:
  — Who are the key characters in the film? Describe each.
  — What organizations are being portrayed? What are some characteristics of the organizations?
  — What organizational problems does the film illustrate? What are factors that led to the problems? How are the problems resolved?
  — How might *Conrack's* situation have been handled differently? What might have happened?
- View the film.
- React to and discuss the impact of the film.
- Discuss the preceding questions and other questions that might be raised.
- Compare *Conrack* and the Choate County Textbook Controversy case study. Identify organizational characteristics and behaviors that are similar or different.
- Relate the case to the readings. Ask participants to identify major points made by the authors in Part I and to locate illustrations of those points in the film.

---

*20th Century Fox, 1973. Martin Ritt, director. Jon Voight, Hume Cronyn, Paul Winfield, Madge Sinclair—cast. 107 min.

- Conclude the film discussion. Summarize the key concepts which participants have discussed and refer them to the author's analysis of the film which is contained in Activity 2. End with a reaction to the author's analysis.

The Film in Brief

To a small isolated island off the coast of South Carolina, untouched by modern technology or education, comes a white idealistic teacher with a briefcase full of unorthodox teaching methods for his black, grade school students. Realizing traditional education methods will fail, he initiates the unusual. All of this, however, doesn't sit too well with the crusty old superintendent who knows just how to deal with teachers who revolt against the established system and "traditional method."

The teacher is Pat Conroy, a youthful, cockey Southern male who has only recently rid himself of an ugly racial prejudice that permeates the community and region. His pupils are silent and obedient, but they cannot count, and they seem to have had few of the experiences that most children take for granted. When the kids cannot pronounce his name correctly, he accepts their pronunciation: " 'Conrack' is close enough."

He is introduced to his class by the principal, a black, middle-aged woman who "knows colored people." She reminds the "colored babies" that they are slow and lazy. Her advice to Conroy: "Treat them tough" because, "they must be taught to please the man."

But, Conroy has his own ideas, and he doesn't "hold with machine education." To shake their docility, he uses banter, horseplay, movies, records, field trips, and campfire chats. He makes false statements to test their alertness and gullibility. To stem a rash of drownings, he teaches the kids to swim. He tutors a man who has never been off the island; and he supports a child who is ridiculed by his peers. The universal themes of music and literature become a source of his lessons.

But the superintendent, used to order and obedience, is suspicious. He has received complaints from "someone" in the community. There is a showdown when Conroy is denied permission to take the kids to a small city on the nearby mainland to celebrate Halloween. He takes them anyway, and consequently is fired for insubordination. The parents support him, but they have no power in the white-controlled school district, and the court upholds the superintendent's decision. The movie closes with the kids at dockside playing Beethoven's Fifth Symphony on a portable phonograph, as they watch Conroy's boat leave the dock.

For its dramatic qualities this movie must be classified as one of the most moving and convincing stories ever filmed about public education. It is realistically composed and tells a powerful, poignant story. The characters are convincingly portrayed in three-dimensional human qualities which make it clear that they act as they do, not because they are good or evil people, but because they are part of a crushing social structure.

The *New York Post* said: "A very touching story, the more so because quite clearly, it's true."

Nora Sayre of the *New York Times* wrote: "The picture revives the hopes and frustrations of the nineteen-sixties, including the idea that deprived people may be nourished by education—a notion that many prefer to neglect today. . . . Jon Voight's performance has a conviction that suggests that the theme of the movie matters a great deal to him. And he deserved special credit for acting with the 21 children selected from a local school—who could snatch a scene from any seasoned actors."

Director: Martin Ritt
Cast: Jon Voight, Hume Cronyn, Paul Winfield, Madge Sinclair
Studio: 20th Century Fox, 1973
Price: $2.00 PG
107 min: (C) CS-r AYC A 2.
Films, Inc.

CONRACK—A FILM ANALYSIS

Roy A. Edelfelt
Ronald G. Corwin

With stark realism this film depicts how the traditions and structure of a community can impinge on a school and ultimately shape the classroom. The hierarchy itself reflects the values of the region. Although the principal is black, she has been co-opted. She is an educated black who remains a figurehead, one who has adopted the attitudes of the white power structure. She is loyal to the system, and even emulates the superintendent's authoritarian, paternalistic style of leadership. Judging from the fate of Conroy, it is easy to speculate about how this individual was favored by the promotion system.

However, the principal is also a person, and must contend with other roles. She is portrayed as a human being with sincere feelings for the children in this community. Her public behavior, in front of the children, contrasts with her informal conversation with Conroy, where she confides that she believes she is simply being realistic about the chances of these children. She wants "her babies" to survive the "snakepit" that will be their world by learning to conform. But the viewer detects that, even though she knows Conroy will fail, she secretly admires his optimism and determination as she encourages him to take his case to the courts.

The authoritarian superintendent was also obviously hand picked for this community. He can be personable and friendly, but his job is to see that teachers obey the system. We do not see the community leaders to whom he is responsible, but they are surely there. His position of authority in the school system means more than being at the top of the hierarchy. He is expected to represent particular citizens in the community and thus is subordinate to their will. His job may be easier because he personally subscribes to the leaders' values, but whether he agrees or not, he must protect their interests to preserve his own position. When Conroy challenges community norms and the superintendent's authority, the superintendent has little choice except to intercede.

The film takes place in the 1960's, an era of upheaval, disillusionment and rapid social change, which in the South was spearheaded by the black-power movement. The film portrays the interdependence of paternalistic, traditional authority and bureaucratic, legal authority. When tradition is challenged by events, the strategic weapons of bureaucracy are brought into play. The curriculum and the rules of the system traditionally kept this particular school in line with the larger system, but when these mechanisms broke down, the principal and then the superintendent directly intervened—first with close supervision, and ultimately by employing the full sanctions of administration to hire, fire and promote, to maintain a loyal and subservient staff.

But, even in this tightly run school system, remember that Conroy was able to do many of the things that he wanted to do. He had a great deal of latitude as long as his actions were confined to the school and not clearly visible to the white power structure of the larger community. This slippage was permitted in part by the fact that this school was isolated from the rest of the district, but it was also tolerated until Conroy's actions became so blatantly visible that the superintendent was forced to take official action. The film demonstrates, then, how structural looseness can be shaped by community norms and public knowledge.

One could say that in the division of labor the superintendent was concerned with the political dimensions of education, while Conroy was concerned with the social purpose of education and pedagogy. But that would be a gross oversimplification. It is true that Conroy seemed to have a better grasp of the academic goals than either the principal or the superintendent, but in showing the children that the system can be challenged, Conroy was also taking a political position. There are political dimensions to any pedagogical method. And, in exposing the children to viewpoints that were at odds with those of the community, Conroy was exposing them to political considerations and hence to some risk. He was helping them to prepare to live a life elsewhere, but for those who were to remain, what Conroy tried to teach them might have made their lives more difficult, as the principal recognizes. It is not just a question of who will benefit from this particular organization, the community or the children, but what course of action will benefit whom. Thus, the film touches a universal dilemma in teaching: whether (or how) to prepare children for a safe and routine life, or to encourage them to accept risk; to prepare them for the here and now, or for an unknown future.

And the question is: who shall decide? That question is answered in the film. It is decided not by the parents who constitute the majority of constituents for this particular school, but by a small but dominant group of white leaders in another community of the district. The film provides portraits of a few black leaders—parents who are respected by their peers. They exercise some leadership, and they make a feeble attempt to support Conroy, but everyone knows that this black majority will be helpless before the white power structure of the school district.

In the final analysis the film demonstrates the folly of an individual attempting to rebel against entrenched bureaucracy. Were there alternatives to rebellion? Could Conroy have achieved his objectives without being fired? Should he have moved more slowly? What alternatives and strategies could he have used? A small nucleus of parent support did develop, but he did not seem able to capitalize on it. Were there other tactics he could have taken? Conroy is a lone teacher. Should he have built a constituency before challenging the system? There was no teacher organization evident in the film that he could call upon. Were there other sources of power at his disposal? Or were there options to rebelling? Could he have used other innovative ways to achieve his goals? The film raises these questions. It does not answer them. But the film can serve as stimulus for discussion along these lines.

Activity 3
Alternate Concepts of Power and Leadership

AN ILLUSTRATION FOR DISCUSSION

"Alternate Concepts of Power and Leadership" is a brief reading which is intended to stimulate participant discussion about the concept of authority by first referring to a description of authority among the Fox Indians. After reading the description participants may want to discuss:
- A definition of authority;
- Authority as it was exercised among the Fox;
- Authority as it is exercised in America's public schools; and
- The author's message to teachers' organizations.

ALTERNATE CONCEPTS OF POWER AND LEADERSHIP

Frankie Beth Nelson

"What is authority?" is an audacious question to raise because of the scope of the question and the risk of deterioration into abstractions that do not represent living people. Some of the concrete reality to which the concept refers has been captured in Walter Miller's comparison of the concept of authority in two contrasting societies. He juxtaposed the Fox Indians around the time of first European contacts (1650 and after) with United States society in the 1950's as a European-derived, western culture (Miller, 1955).

The Fox was one of eight Central Algonkian tribes that lived in the Great Lakes region. In the mid-17th century they practiced an animistic religion that especially contrasts with western religions in the matter of the relationship between humans and gods, which the Fox referred to as *manitu.** The Fox did not place their gods up in the sky higher than and superior to humans, as westerners do. Rather, these gods were to be found in the four corners of the universe on the same plane as people. One of their important gods, Wisakeya, was addressed as "my nephew"—a basically egalitarian kin term instead of the more ponderous "our father". No Fox deities were considered objects of "hallowed respect, adoration or worshipful deference" according to Miller (281). Each male Fox would have courted his own god at adolescence while on a vision quest. He did this while fasting alone in the forest for four days

---

**According to Miller, manitu was "... a kind of generalized essence of supernatural power everywhere and available to everyone," although no one had it forever. When one succeeded at something, one was considered to have had manitu power, just as failure was interpreted to mean that one had lost it. Although any person or thing became a manitu while behaving powerfully, the manitu power was held conditionally and temporarily (279).*

and nights, until a *manitu* appeared and revealed how the boy could control the power of the *manitu,* detailing the obligations to be fulfilled by the boy in this reciprocal relationship. The god was accepted if the youth believed that the power would work well for him. For this discussion of authority, the most interesting symbol of the Fox was their notion that the afterlife was a place "where the sun goes down . . . over yonder" where good people did "whatever they please," whereas the wicked when they died had to obey a *manitu.* Miller believes that they equated hell with being told what to do (282). We only have mythic evidence for their supernatural belief about taking orders, but the horrified Europeans who first observed them left little doubt that taking orders was most objectionable to the Fox. Miller reports that they were considered "insubordinate," "disobedient," and "undisciplined" (271-272).

Nor was heroism a part of their culture—fellow human beings were not accorded "special, mystic, hallowed qualities of supreme power, supernatural grace, and ultimate infallibility" (282). A chief in a Fox village inherited his role, but the office did not involve any "directive authority" (253). Direction of other people did figure more in the role of war-leader than was the case with the village chief. The post of war-leader was held during single warring excursions of only a few days' duration, with never more than 15 men choosing to join the war-leader, and leaving whenever he displeased them (285). Before a war-leader could re-enter his village, he had to participate in a ritual that revoked his authority, thus cleansing himself of the dangers to others of his power. Rather than admiring powerful beings, god or human, the Fox feared them.

The egalitarian nature of Fox society was also apparent in the manner in which they reared their children. They socialized the children too thoroughly to need authoritarian control. Their goal was for the children to constrain and control themselves, obeying the rules through the inner conviction of conscience rather than from outer coercion. Sons respected their fathers relative to age as did junior to senior kin, but did not obey them. Those same early European observers were amazed that Fox fathers did not punish their children for such offenses as stealing and lying, but instead "reasoned" and "taught" the negative consequences such as "loss of luck and reputation," or occasionally made them fast— "the closest thing to corporal punishment that properly occurs." (Tax, 1955) Miller offers an intriguing explanation of the father-son equality. He believes that the "internalized symbol of moral authority (superego) does not exist in Fox." Superego in the Fox personality is quite different from our own dynamics of conscience formation. The Fox resolve the Oedipal conflict through the symbolism of the vision quest where there is ritual enactment of a definitive severance of dependency. Symbolically, the adolescent dies and, when born again, is protected by the powerful *manitu* that he has found for himself. Instead of the internalization of the father, as in western myth and Freudian theory, the *manitu* guardian performs the conscience functions of the personality (287).

An order, whether given by a Fox adult to a child, by a war leader to a member of the war party, or by a ceremony leader to someone participating in the ritual, was deemed an insult because of the implication that the individual being ordered did not know the rules, or could not adequately perform in keeping with Fox tradition. From the perspective of our culture where none of us knows the rules and procedures for any segment other than our own, it is of some note that all of the Fox knew how every part of the culture worked—partly through repetition, partly because of the small scale of the society and the operational consequence that there was no secretiveness about the rules and procedures. There was no hiding of rules to deny access to any status, since there was very little differentiation. For example, there were no rules for upper-class grammatical usage as in "Pygmalion." Not only did power convey no right to order someone else, it was available to all, conceptualized as unlimited, constantly being won and lost by any one individual whether god or human. Fox gods, just like their human clients, rather frequently lost their power in encounters with others who had stronger *manitu*.

Miller's portrait of the Fox concept of authority is all the more telling because he has translated it for us into the realm of what he has called "personal attitude" and concrete behavior (283). He also gives us the historical sources of some of the personal as well as person-to-person attitudes that are implicit in our own concept of authority. The European derivation of authority is apparent in Miller's description of the lord-serf relationship of sixth-century England, the Jesuit superior-priest relation of sixteenth-century Spain and the French king-subject relation of the seventeenth century. He analyzes the six features that are characteristic of all three relationships:

- an individual empowered to direct someone else,
- a depersonalization of the relationship from man-to-man to that of role-to-role,
- permanent empowerment of the "superior" role,
- allocation of higher status to the dominator,
- passive acceptance by the individual holding the "inferior" position, and
- differential access to rules.

Although we do not now practice the slavish deference to royalty that was characteristic of a millenium ago in Europe, we cannot ignore the history of such past events as they subtly influence our present-day person-to-person behavior. One conjectures that we condone various undemocratic practices in our schools because we reassure ourselves we are not as bad as our predecessors.

Miller points out that western relations of authority give one individual the power to direct the actions of another, who is obligated to obey. Conditioned as we are to thinking that "what is" is normal, we believe that "of course," the "superior" gives orders "down" a chain of command to an "inferior." Unlike the Fox, whose belief that powerful roles should be temporary led them to divest authority from war leaders, we often make power roles permanent. Even more repugnant to the Fox would be the association of greater prestige with power which we semantically designate as "superior." In our society as the subordinated defers to his designated superior his acceptance makes the difference seem natural or basic. The "superior" because he knows how to proceed, is conceptualized as director of the activity of the deferring "inferior" who has been held in ignorance of the procedures and rules. The middle class functions in symbiosis with a social class to which it can feel superior. If it is going to win status symbols it has been conditioned to value, there must be visible losers in order to define the winners.

Our society accepts as "normal and necessary," according to Miller, such role relations entailing authority as "boss-employee, teacher-pupil, parent-child, foreman-worker, pastor-parishioner, orchestra leader-sideman, coach-team member, director-cast member, captain-crew member, doctor-patient, chief-staff member." Miller suggests that the occupant of the "superior" status derives his expectation of being obeyed from the symbolic power of rationalized superiority. We take this matter so much for granted that we fail to question the way we think about it. There is cultural consensus that a "superior (should) . . . direct the actions of another (who is) . . . obligated to accept that direction." Organizational specialists refer to this as "vertical authority" and represent it as a hierarchy or a pyramid (275).

What insights can be gained from Miller's comparison of Fox and American concepts of authority that bear upon teacher organizations?

The small scale of Fox society (probably never more than a few thousand in population) made possible a close web of primary relationships where one cannot evade the consequences of one's actions. The complex organizations of our society, however benign the benefits attributed to them, do not compensate for the context of knowing others so thoroughly that determining the truth value of their statements is possible. Efforts to restore this face-to-face, person-to-person context seem more sentimental than wise. Perhaps they only seem so, because they have been done in bad faith. I refer to the attempts at decentralization of large bureaucratic organizations that give the appearance of reallocating power while merely making secret its real location under the cover of obfuscation and confusion. One hopes that teachers' organizations will reflect the sophistication of the members and try to invent a form of organization that will in good faith really diffuse power and preserve the integrity which is a product of primary relations. The desire for efficiency and expediency often takes priority over the openness that "ought" to be a part of public proceedings.

Perhaps we already imitate the Fox with regard to individualistic religion. My students make such statements as these:

"My god is. . .

'. . . something I feel inside myself,'

'... raised consciousness of life,'
'... only a matter of chance formulated to make up my fate.' "

Although four days and four nights of fasting might render the *manitu* more profound, the statements are as full of individualism as they are lacking in moral content. The great western religions once provided the moral power of our society. Freudian theorists such as Donald McIntosh (1970) believe that through religion, individuals externalize their prerational thoughts about omnipotent parents by projecting those feelings onto a god or gods. He says that a god is a metaphor for a "basic self-acceptance." (905) Whether moral power be sacred or secular, our sixth-, sixteenth-, and seventeenth-century forefathers built in an authority process of domination and coercion. The moral right to dominate and coerce others, in which teachers believe they are clothed, is not apparent to everyone everywhere. Instead, we are found as naked in our "bossiness" as when the early European explorers ordered the Fox, when we teach foreigners, or even children, whose disruptive shouts contradict the invisible cloak of the right to coerce which is not apparent just because one party is called "teacher" and the other "pupil."

When Pandora's box of cultural pluralism was let loose, we became a nation with an authority crisis because the legitimating rationale of permanent dominance of an "inferior" by a "superior" was shown to be the coercive domination that is so galling to the imputed "inferior." As teachers, probably through their collective power in organizations, move out of their compliant, establishment-oriented, norm-supporting stance of a generation ago, I hope that they will strike a courageous attitude. The dual principles of authority are the opposite poles of power and truth. Wherever teaching and teachers have influenced culture, they have demonstrated the moral power of truth over the power of force and coercion, whether "legitimate" or not.

REFERENCES

McIntosh, Donald. Weber and Freud on the nature and sources of authority. *American Sociological Review*, October 1970, *35*, 901-911.

Miller, Walter B. Two concepts of authority. *American Anthropologist*, February 1955, *57*, 271-289.

Tax, Sol. The social organization of the Fox Indians. In Fred Eggan (Ed.), *Social anthropology of North American Indian tribes*, enlarged edition. Chicago: University of Chicago Press, 1955 (1939). Pp. 243-284.

Activity 4
Ethnomethodology

In the three volumes of this series we have attempted not only to demonstrate that it is important for each of us to become better informed about how organizations function, but also to acquaint the reader with a variety of perspectives and approaches that can be used for this purpose. Because life in complex organizations is multifaceted, there are no simple explanations. Each of us needs to learn to use the rich variety of concepts, methods of analyses, and modes of learning that are available. We have seen that films, case studies, vignettes, essays, and other means can all assist.

With this in mind, we turn now to a little known but provocative method that any interested student can profitably use to expose the (often obscure) assumptions underlying this organizational society. The method is called "ethnomethodology." Don't be intimidated by the tongue-twisting term. It refers to something all can comprehend: *how people make sense out of their everyday worlds*. It is an absorbing, arresting approach which can yield surprising insights into routine events that most people take for granted.

This method and some of its implications are discussed in the following paper by Laurel Walum. The author also provides examples of techniques that can be employed with the method, which are supplemented with a few additional suggestions from Donald R. Cruickshank. Walum's discussion includes a thoughtful analysis of how various techniques relate to cultural differences and can be used to unmask some of our (often rather insidious) ethnocentric beliefs.

We encourage the reader to try this approach, and perhaps invent still other harmless exercises that illuminate features of organizations.

For the student who is interested in exploring this approach further, Walum has suggested some additional readings.

A SHORT NOTE ON ETHNOMETHODOLOGY

Laurel Richardson Walum

Ethnomethodology has its theoretical roots in the phenomenological tradition: the understanding of social reality from the point of view of the meaning it has for the actor. Ethnomethodology assumes that the understanding of social life cannot be accomplished by the imposition of natural science assumptions and methodologies because humans are not just objects to be observed. Rather, it assumes humans are active in the creation of their cultural worlds, therefore, understanding of social life must take into account the meaning a social act has for the actor.

The term "ethnomethodology," coined by Harold Garfinkel, simply means the "methods"—means, techniques, procedures, etc.—by which people, "ethno-", go about constructing social reality—making sense—in their everyday lives. Thus, the ethnomethodologist is concerned with discovering what those methods are as well as the nature of the realities that are constructed. For example, if an ethnomethodologist were studying how a jury knows it has made a correct decision, he or she would focus on how the *jurors* approach a verdict, how *they* decide what is relevant to the verdict, how *they* determine criteria to use, what those criteria are, and therefore, how *they* know they have reached a correct verdict. That is, the problem is understanding how persons make sense out of their worlds.

Although the American society is culturally pluralistic, most organizations within it are based on the cultural assumptions of white middle-class America, and most persons who control these organizations share those assumptions by virtue of childhood or adult socialization into white middle class. However, because of our cultural diversity, persons who work at various levels within these organizations bring different assumptions about the meanings of the behaviors that they observe and exhibit within the organization. One consequence is that members may inadvertently violate the organizational norms, and the violation may result in negative sanctioning that extends well beyond the particular norm violation—for example, a generalized lowered evaluation of the members' contributions to the organization. A second consequence is that members from different cultural backgrounds may feel uncomfortable and/or rewarded because they are unfamiliar with the rules of the organization and the reward structure.

Because the number of cultures within our society is great, rather than focus on only one or two of them, participants are asked to draw on their own understandings based on their own regional, ethnic, class, and sex backgrounds. The major areas of cultural diversity to explore didactically are space, time, and language.

Because much of what persons use in creating cultural sense depends on what they take for granted ("routine grounds of everyday behavior") and do not recognize as operating rules, one of the major tasks of the ethnomethodologist has been to develop demonstration techniques or procedures by which this everyday, taken-for-granted cultural world can be made visible. The techniques/procedures that follow are grounded in this ethnomethodological perspective and are intended to make visible to the participants some "taken-for-granteds" about social organizations. Only by understanding these primary "taken-for-granteds" can the participants move to an understanding of organizations at the macrolevel.

The techniques/procedures are organized around the teaching/learning of certain concepts in the area of social organization. For each concept, suggested procedures and expected learnings are provided. The material is not intended to be used exactly as written; rather, it is a pedagogical guide. Where detailed questions or descriptions are given, the purpose is to increase the instructor's fund of resources rather than to prescribe a style of presentation.

SUGGESTED EXERCISE

Exercise 1. Learning about Superordinate-Subordinate Relationships Within Social Contexts

Superordinate Role

PROCEDURE. It is assumed that the setting is a classroom, meeting room, or the like. The instructor comes to the front and engages in common-sense instructor-type behavior; for example, he or she introduces him- or herself, greets the participants, or picks up the chalk. The instructor then interrupts him- or herself and queries the members, "How do you know I belong up here? How do you know I am who I say I am? How do you know I am the instructor/teacher? How do you know I am leading this set of learnings?" *Query and probe:* Seek common-sense understandings of what the role is and how it is recognized. Use *imaginative reconstruction:* "What if I had refused to come up here? Or what if once up here, I refused to talk?" Probe for normative understandings, such as the leader stands in front, asks questions, addresses the participants, and begins and terminates interaction; the leader acts authoritatively. He or she has the right to choose which questions to ask, which subject matter to discuss, how it will be pursued, etc.; and he or she has the obligation to do the above. That is, the right and obligation to lead are communicated through activity that is recognizable.

LEARNING. We are able to recognize authority figures (superordinates) because they behave in ways that convince us they are who they claim to be; they act in terms of a set of *rights* and *obligations* that we take for granted as belonging to superordinates. They are seen as having the legitimate right to process interaction and the obligation to do so.

Subordinate Role

PROCEDURE. *Query and probe:* "How do I know that you're the audience? How do I know that you are who you claim to be? How do you yourselves know? What do you do to convince yourselves and me that you are learners-subordinates?" Continue questioning and probing to elicit as much common-sense material as possible concerning the taken-for-granteds surrounding the subordinate role—behavior such as sitting, waiting, answering questions, and expecting to be asked questions as well as "nonbehavior," not throwing chalk, not swinging on doors, etc.

LEARNING. We are able to recognize the subordinate role because subordinates act in ways that convince us that they are who they claim to be; they act in terms of a set of rights and obligations that we take for granted as belonging to subordinates. We share knowledge of these rights and obligations as common cultural carriers of standard America.

OPTIONAL EXTENDING PROCEDURE. The instructor may wish to pursue these cues to superordinate and subordinate roles within different subcultures. That is, how do subcultures and ethnic groups differ in their understandings of behavior that signals a super- or subordinate role?

Superordinate-Subordinate Role Reciprocity

PROCEDURE. *Query and probe:* "Can I perform my role as leader without you? Can you perform your roles without me? What if I weren't here? What if no one were here?" Probe for imaginative reconstruction of what would happen if authority were not present (for example, the class would leave) and what would happen if subordinates were not there (for example, the professor would leave). That is, "Would I know who I was— would I still be who I claimed to be if others did not acknowledge through their taken-for-granteds that I was who I claimed to be?" Can subordinates claim to be who they are without the authority figure? Review earlier discussion. Behavior, cues, norms, and expectations for subordinates are the reciprocals of those for the superordinate.

LEARNING. The roles of superordinate and subordinate are *reciprocal.* Performance of one requires performance of the other. The rights of the superordinate carry obligations for the subordinate; the obligations of the superordinate carry rights for the subordinate.

OPTIONAL EXTENDING PROCEDURE. The instructor may wish to explore this role reciprocity in terms of other role networks, for example, foreman-worker, team leader-member, or father-child. The basic role-reciprocity relationships between superordinates and subordinates may be generalized across different organizational settings.

Superordinate-Subordinate Relationships Within a Social Context

PROCEDURE. *Query and probe:* "What is our present 'social context'? What is this event we are living/creating? How do we know we are in a staff-training (teacher-training) event?" Probe for common-sense understandings—cues from the environment (spatial, visual, tactile—for example, persons sitting in chairs); the existence of administrative personnel; the pieces of paper that told everyone the context, the mood, etc.

Probe and ask for earlier experiences on which this "creative interpretation" is based, that is, sitting in these sessions before, having experience with the teachers before, etc. Probe for the kind of superordinate-subordinate relationship existing in the room that signals that this is a social context for "learning."

LEARNING. Superordinate-subordinate relationships take place in social contexts that are recognizable to the participants. Social organization is *contextually* based.

PROCEDURE. Norm violation: The instructor violates a particular norm known to govern superordinate-subordinate relationships in this context. For example, he or she throws chalk on the floor, leaves the room, turns his or her back on the class, begins discussing poetry with one particular student, goes to the rear of the room and talks to the wall, or does a jig. (The norm chosen for violation should be one comfortable for the instructor, appropriate for the particular class, and observable by all class members.) *Query and probe:* "What happened? What did I do?" Probe for explanations that rationalize a seemingly inappropriate activity within this setting; for example, "You're trying to teach us something," "You did it to get our attention better," or "You're not crazy—you had a reason." That is, persons will not know what happened until they have interpreted it; and those interpretations will be within the context of the setting. Because this context is a "learning/educational" one, they will look for pedagogical explanations and interpretations of the behavior. *Query and probe:* "What if I were outside and did what I just did (for example, broke a piece of chalk and threw it down or talked to the wind)? How would you interpret that?" Probe the relevance of the setting. Suggest other settings and ask how the behavior might be interpreted.

LEARNING. We do not only take for granted the rights and obligations of role performers in a social context, but we interpret their behaviors to be meaningful within that context. In some contexts, the superordinate may violate the norms—act outside the rules—with impunity; and such behavior is interpreted (rationalized) in the context of the *situation*.

Exercise 2. Learning about Rule-Based Behavior

Normative Understandings about Rules Taken for Granted

PROCEDURE. Norm violation (modification of a demonstration used by Harold Garfinkel): The instructor draws a grid of two horizontal parallel lines and two vertical parallel lines (a tic-tac-toe grid). Without stating the purpose of the grid, the instructor picks up the chalk and asks, "Who wants to play?" (Do not use the words tic-tac-toe.) The instructor places an "X" in a box, the volunteer an "O," and so on until it appears that the volunteer might win. At that point, the instructor erases one of the volunteer's "O's" and inserts an "X" (and several others if necessary), draws the diagonal line to signify "I win," and waits. Most likely, the volunteer will shrug and say, "Okay, you win;" alternatively, the volunteer may erase the instructor's moves or start a different grid and win, etc. *Query and probe:* "What happened?" Probable responses are that the instructor cheated, didn't follow the rules, etc. Probe: "Why do you say I cheated? What makes you think I was playing tic-tac-toe? I thought I was playing toe-tac-tic. How did you know I was playing tic-tac-toe?" Probe the symbol of the grid and with it the set of assumed rules that govern the play. Probe the assumption that everyone understood and was following the same set of rules.

LEARNING. We share a set of expectations regarding *rules* governing not just games, but our social interaction. We assume on the basis of symbols and cues that the rules are shared among the members.

OPTIONAL EXTENDED LEARNINGS. The instructor may wish to discuss subculture variations or situations in which different sets of rules are assumed by different groups.

OPTIONAL EXTENDING PROCEDURE. The instructor may wish to link this tic-tac-toe game directly back to the superordinate-subordinate role relationship, either as a substitute for the procedure suggested there or as a follow-up reconfirming experience (reconfirmation of the role of the superordinate within a social context). *Query and probe:* "Why did I do that? What were my reasons? Why was I able to? What if I had done that at a party?"

Exercise 3. Normative Understandings About Rules of Common Sense, Logic, and Rationality

PROCEDURE. (Modification of a didactic tool suggested by Harvey Sachs.) The group is told that it is going to play "Twenty Questions." One member is asked to volunteer to be the questioner. When the volunteer is out of the room, the group is instructed that (a) it will have nothing in mind for the volunteer to guess, (b) it will be programmed to answer questions in the sequence "yes-yes-no" (or "yes-no"), and (c) it should pay special attention to how the volunteer tries to make sense out of nothing. The volunteer returns and, as the game progresses, is asked to explain out loud why he or she is asking particular questions. (The instructor may have to intervene and encourage a fuller explanation.) (In all my experiences with this technique the volunteer has never failed to construct a logical-rational sequence out of what appear to be contradictory responses and to finally get a "yes" to a specific, "It is X.")

Discussion should follow on the kinds of methods the volunteer used—the rules he or she was taking for granted, for example, that there was an object, that the answers were honest, and that logical deductions and narrowing the universe would succeed in finding the answer.

LEARNING. We assume that the world is meaningful and use that assumption to make sense out of it when none may exist. We assume that rules are followed by others around us. We assume that logical, rational thought will provide correct information. We act in terms of rule-governed behavior within social contexts.

Exercise 4. Learning about Status Cues across Organizations

PURPOSE. In this series of suggested procedures, the intention is to sensitize persons to the taken-for-granted cultural cues carried as standard American baggage within organizations and interpersonally to maintain a status hierarchy, a communication network, and specialization.

PROCEDURES. The staff may choose to illustrate the cultural clues (to be discussed below) through norm violations, discussion, or imaginative reconstruction (the "What-if?" question). (In my own experience, at least some violation of norms is necessary in order for the learning to take place. I would suggest choosing some and simply mentioning the others.)

The instructor should explain the purpose of the learning segment: to illustrate and understand how verbal and nonverbal behavior conveys cues to others concerning one's status. This area of sociolinguistics is newly being explored, and therefore, following are only some of the cues that are used and interpreted in standard American organizations. The staff may wish to explore other status cues as well as discuss status cues that operate in subcultures. Particular attention may be paid to how these subcultural status cues might prove threatening to the status of persons in an organizational hierarchy that depends on standard American cues for maintaining distance and boundaries.

PROXEMICS. Proxemics is the use of space to convey meaning. Some examples to discuss (or to violate) are:

1. The higher a person's status in an organization or social setting, the greater the space alloted. For example, an instructor has the whole front of the room and a large desk; students sit row by row, equidistant from each other. Principals have private offices; teachers have private desks and closets; students (in high school) share desks and only have private lockers. In universities, the president, provost, deans, chairpersons, full professors, associate professors, assistant professors, and teaching assistants are provided with differing amounts of space in a descending order.

2. Persons of higher status can invade the space of those of lower status, but not vice versa. For example, men are accorded greater personal space than women. When speaking distance is measured between male and male, male and female, and female and female, it is evident that less distance is provided for the female (that is, her personal space can be invaded).
3. There are culturally understood "correct" distances between persons. In standard America the distance for conversation is two to four feet. If one person violates the norms of correct speaking distance by standing too close, the other's sense of propriety is enraged; or if one person stands too far away, the other perceives a lack of interest.
4. The higher-status person may initiate physical contact with the lower-status person, but not vice versa. "Touch" is really the final invasion of personal space. Females are touched more frequently in more places by males than vice versa. Priests touch supplicants, doctors touch patients, coaches touch football players, teachers touch students, etc.

CHRONEMICS. Chronemics refers to the use of time to convey meaning. Some ideas to pursue with the interns are the following:
1. Standard American organizations assume that time is meaningful; a scheduled event is to take place at the scheduled time. What does it imply to be late for an appointment? Not to show up? To arrive a day early? To arrive several hours early? What are subcultural variations/presumptions about time? What is meant by "black man's time"?
2. Time (or timing) is also crucial to processing interaction and conveying one's status. Normative rules govern pauses/spaces/understandings related to when someone has relinquished the floor and when he or she has not. What happens if you violate these norms? What happens if you allow long silences (you do not respond)? What happens when you interrupt someone who has not stopped speaking? What happens when you continue talking while someone else is talking?
3. In general, the higher the status, the greater the right to timing. The higher-status person interrupts more frequently (men interrupt women more than women interrupt men), can choose the chronemic device for the interaction (um. . um. . um. . or nonstop lecture), can keep the lower-status person waiting (in doctor's offices, in welfare agencies, at teacher's desks, etc.), can change the time of the meeting, can control the amount of time to be spent on the issue, etc.
4. In hierarchical organizations, a "correct" ordering of interaction requires communication through "the proper chain of command." What happens if you go to the top first rather than up the chain? What happens if you go to the top first if you are not a member of an organization in contrast to if you are? Can you tell who has what position in an organization by whom they talk to and in what order the communications flow?

5. How does the order in which information flows (who finds out what, when) provide clues to a person's position in an informal status hierarchy?
6. What meaning is conveyed by changing the speed of speech? For example, what consequences for information-seeking does talking fast have? Talking too slowly?

KINESICS. Kinesics refers to the conveying of meaning through body movement, posture, eye contact, etc. It is probably the most studied of the nonverbal communication patterns. Some suggested cues to explore are:
1. What body movements indicate equality among organization members? Examples: hand shaking, equalized touching, and mirror-image body postures.
2. What body movements indicate inequality among organization members (that is, differential placement along the hierarchy)? How is deference presented through body language? How is authority presented? Examples: Deference is presented through curtsey, dropped eyes, cocked head, smile, and arms held in toward the body—gestures that make one's "volume" smaller; authority is presented through stance, hands in pockets (a dominance gesture for males), and hands moving in large kinespheres (increased "volume").
3. What body movements indicate that a person's status is being threatened? Examples: moving in to protect territory and swinging one's leg. It might be worth-while to go through some of the standard American metaphors that involve body imagery—"My back is breaking," "I'd give my right arm to . . .," "I'm hitting my head against a brick wall," "You're pulling my leg"—and sensitize the participants to the actual body movements that are nonverbally communicating those sentiments.
4. Facial cues are generally assumed to give better information about a person than body cues. However, because most persons in standard American organizations have learned to control facial expressions, it might be worth focusing on the disjunctions between facial cues and body cues. For example, a stare with the head facing forward indicates dominance; but a stare with a cocked head (tilted to the side) indicates submissiveness; that is, the tilted head undercuts the usual meaning of the stare.

PARALINGUISTICS. Paralinguistics refers to the secondary aspects of speech (that is, not the content or the words), for example, pitch, tone, volume, accent, phrasing, and style. What happens to the processing of information (or the process of communication) when paralinguistic elements are varied? For example, what happens when volume is raised? What happens when it is lowered? What happens when speech is atonal (monotone)? What effects does an accent have on the listener? Will a person with a standard English accent receive different information than one with a subcultural accent? What assumptions are made about persons whose style of speech is "cutesy" or "whiny" or "aggressive"? How do these assumptions affect the kind of quality of information received? How do they affect entry into organizations and placement within them?

ETIQUETTE. Although etiquette is not usually considered an element of nonverbal communication, for the purposes of this training it may be placed here because following the rules of "polite society" conveys to recipient as well as sender that "I am such-and-such kind of person."

1. The staff may want to consider discussing some "common courtesies" that in fact are behavioral demonstrations of status differentials, opening doors for those of lower status, picking up the restaurant tab for lower-status persons, or hailing cabs.

2. The staff may want to consider discussing some "common courtesies" that in fact are behavioral demonstrations of status equality, hand shaking or certain kinds of greetings and leavings. (I suspect that there are very few of these.)

Exercise 5. Cultural Diversity Regarding the Meaning of Space

PROCEDURE. Participants are asked to draw what they would consider a perfect office (or classroom or building).

DISCUSSION. There is considerable cultural variation related to the meaning of space. Some known examples from proxemics studies may help participants understand how their assumptions of privacy-intrusion/distance-conspiracy are related to their own culture's assumptions regarding space. For example, German cultures tend to prefer solid doors and furniture, fixed seating and walls. Middle-class American culture assumes that doors are closed only when privacy is desired. Office space for middle-class Americans stops at the walls; for German and Japanese cultures it extends into the space surrounding the office. Middle-class Americans tend to see themselves as having a right to their own "space" or room or desk, and that space is private and inviolate. Private space is not taken for granted among British-Americans, Japanese, East Indians, and most lower-class ethnic and racial cultures in America. When middle-class Americans want to think or be alone, they provide themselves with architectural barriers, whereas other groups can erect ego barriers that signal to others in the same space, "Don't disturb." The middle-class American perceives such "silent treatments" as rude. In middle-class American organizations, one's position in the hierarchy is determined by the size of the office as well as the number of architectural barriers between the office and the rest of the organization. For example, to see a high-ranking executive, you may have to pass through a reception area, a secretarial staff area, and a private secretary's office before entering the space designated as the executive's. Persons with French cultural background, on the other hand, assume that the person in the middle of the space has the highest status and the important paths are those that emanate outward from the center in starlike fashion.

Japanese culture also assumes that the central position is the important one, but assumes that it can be approached from any direction; that is, the intersection of points is important, not the routes to these points. Because many routes are possible, architectural features of rooms are seen as artificially fixed, and symbolically limiting the activities of the organization and the flow of interpersonal relationships. Arab cultures accept close physical proximity with people, but consider architecturally obstructed spaces (and no views) to be ego invasions.

Query: What is assumed from your cultural backgrounds about the meaning of space? What do arrangements of persons, objects, and walls mean to you? What assumptions do you make about closed doors? What assumptions do you make about persons of the opposite sex being together behind closed doors? How do those assumptions limit your perspective about the role of women in organizations? What assumptions do you make about the amount of space which you are entitled to? How is your morale enhanced or deflated by the space accorded you? What assumptions do you make about persons who "invade" your space—or those whom you perceive as remaining "distant"?

LEARNING. Spatial arrangements are culturally learned. We carry our culture's assumptions about the meaning of the use of space into organizations. We define ourselves, others, and the organization in terms of spatial messages.

Exercise 6. Cultural Diversity Regarding the Meaning of Time

Standard American organizations assume that time is important, and they tend to schedule events tightly. Swiss, German, Japanese, and black-American cultures tend to allow more time between appointments and to assume interpersonal relationships are an important component.

Query: What does your culture say about scheduling? Is it wasting time to "chat"? Are the tasks more important than the persons with whom the tasks are to be shared? Is it "rude" to just get down to business? Is it "unprofessional" (or uncommitted to the organization) to leave promptly at 5:00 p.m.? What consequences do your cultural beliefs and practices have on the organization? What effects do the organization's preferences for schedules have on its evaluation of your contribution and commitment?

Standard white middle-class organizations assume that time is to be treated monochromatically; that is, one thing is to be scheduled *after* another in some kind of orderly sequence. Such monochromatic assumptions are usually also associated with compartmentalization of activities and low interpersonal involvement. Persons from southern European cultural backgrounds, on the other hand, tend to treat time polychromatically; that is, they keep many activities going simultaneously and maintain high levels of interpersonal involvement. (Architecturally such assumptions are reflected in the strung-out Main Streets of America in contrast to the plazas and piazzas of southern Europe.

Query: What does your culture assume about how to "use time"? Does it seem as though "nothing is getting done" when many tasks are going on simultaneously? Do you assume that persons with low status (for example women) are polychromatic? How can organizations take account of these differences? Are there ways to use space to synchronize time? For example, what happens when a symbol of low interpersonal involvement is exchanged for a symbol of high interpersonal involvement such as sitting on a couch to have a discussion?

LEARNING. Time is culturally defined and carries different meanings for persons of different cultures.

Exercise 7. Cultural Diversity Regarding the Meaning of Talk

Talk fulfills different functions for different cultures and different assumptions are made about the importance of talk, depending on who is talking to whom. Within most organizations, there is an assumption that the relevance of the talk is directly proportional to the organizational status of the communicants. For example, it is assumed that male executives interacting by the pure-water machine are engaged in "shop talk" whereas female secretaries are engaged in "girl talk."

Within the black culture, talk is used for many purposes, and effective speech is important. Black males achieve status within the community through their ability to use language creatively and competitively. Consequently, black males tend to talk frequently, lyrically, and actively, and tend to expect feedback that urges the continuance of the talking "performance." That is, talking is an art and a skill—not just a bit of expressive oil for an instrumental task. Black females, on the other hand, are expected to earn their respectability through their own "talk" and their ability to handle the "talk" of those around them. The use of "talk" for black males and black females is different; but both share a cultural understanding regarding its artfulness and relevance.

Query: How does your culture use "talk"? Do you use talk differently with members of the same sex than with members of the opposite sex? What does your culture say about persons who use talk differently than you do? If you are black, how have you come to interpret the white middle class use of talk? To what extent does maintaining your culture's definition of the use of language create problems for the organization? For the members?

OPTIONAL EXTENDED PROCEDURE. The instructor might ask participants to role play a speech situation within an organization, requesting role players to (a) use talk as it is used in their culture, and (b) use talk as they assume it should be used in a white middle-class organization.

LEARNING. There is cultural diversity regarding the meaning of "talk."

Exercise 8. Learning about Resistance to Change as a (Partial) Function of Acceptance of the Normative Order

PROCEDURE. Review the previous exercises and learnings. The way persons act in their daily lives reconfirms their positions in their organizations. By acting like a person who has a certain position (through verbal and nonverbal cues), you confirm to yourself and others that that is your position. Social organizations have hierarchies, and these hierarchies are reinforced (concretized) through the taken-for-granted acts of persons within them. Therefore, one of the major reasons for nonchange in organizations is the behavioral acceptance of what is.

ASSIGNMENT. Ask participants to violate a norm in some setting other than their present class setting. The norm that they choose to violate should not be questionable ethically, morally, or legally nor reflect poorly on them or the project. Some examples are eating peas with a knife, playing "dumb" (like not knowing the meaning of a common word like gasoline), paying for food purchases with pennies, requesting a nickel's worth of gas, a female entering a barber shop, wearing clothes inside-out, saying "Yes, thank you" in response to all questions, and answering the phone as though you made the call. There are literally thousands of such everyday rules of behavior that we follow. Participants should select one to violate (perhaps one that they have never felt was a "good" norm); caution them not to hurt themselves, others, or the project. Because there are so many everyday rules, there is no reason for them to get elaborate or ethically questionable. It is important that they do the assignment now (within this context) and not report on some norm that they inadvertently (or purposefully) violated in the past. Alternatively, the instructor may wish to propose the same norm violation for the entire class, for example, cutting into a line, paying with pennies, not opening doors for females (if a male) or opening doors for males (if a female), or talking to a stranger in an elevator.

WRITTEN ASSIGNMENT. Participants should write up their norm-violation experience in a brief form (three paragraphs or so). In the report they should include (a) what norm was violated (the setting and context), (b) how others responded, and (c) how they subjectively felt about it. (The last is important to include: Some will report feeling free, some will report feeling awful, and some may not have been able to violate a norm on purpose at all.)

DISCUSSION. Time should be allotted for sharing experiences and discussing why the norm violation was easy or hard, why people noticed or not, etc. Particular emphasis should be placed on how the norms are carried in our heads, but are not necessarily relevant to others. Emphasis should also be placed on the idea that participants acted as individuals. *Query:* Would it have been easier to have been part of a group? (This discussion should lead into the following exercise on strategies for change.)

Exercise 9. Learning about Strategies for Effecting Change

PURPOSE. The purpose of this extended exercise is to provide participants with some alternative strategies and tactics for learning about social change. The approach suggested is experimental; based on their learnings, the participants will explore the consequences on different strategies and tactics for achieving a goal they set for themselves. The exercise does not assume that all strategies and tactics have been catalogued and evaluated. Rather, it is hoped that through this framework of experimental approach, the participants can develop new strategies and tactics and the ability to evaluate them.

PROCEDURES. Participants should be in task groups of five to ten persons. Their task is to choose something within their current environment that they want changed, for example, smoking in the classrooms, racist or sexist practices, lack of garbage cans, or breakfast menus.

[If some exercises in communications are wanted here, participants could focus on the processes by which their group comes to a consensus. (It is suggested that they keep "field notes" of their own task groups.) Attention should be paid to such questions as the division of labor within the group, informal leadership, informal information exchange, coalition formation, instrumental and expressive role specializations, etc.]

Once a problem has been selected, the task groups should consider the following kinds of questions about strategies and tactics to get done what they want accomplished. They might choose to try differing tactics to learn experimentally what effect these tactics have on the outcome.

1. In order to effect change by working through the system, you need to know who is in a position to effect that change. That is, you need to know who within the bureaucracy has the legitimate authority to make decisions in the area in question. How do you go about finding out whom you should communicate with? Possible tactics and strategies: the phone book, informal asking, looking for the "formal" authority or an "information" leader. Participants might want to experiment with different chains of information gathering—for example, asking the campus information operator and following

the probable flow of calls from there; using the campus director, choosing several likely sources, and following the flow; or going to an ombudsperson, asking informally who is knowledgeable about "X" area, and seeking information from those persons. Participants may want to keep records of their objective activities, their subjective responses (anger, rage, frustration, etc.), and how the subjective responses are handled within the group (for example, do persons specializing in "feeling-catharsis" develop?).

2. Having located the person or office with responsibility for the area in question, how do you best get access to that person or office?
   a. What effects do individuals as individuals have versus groups? Participants may want to consider experimentally (or in terms of "What if?") the following kinds of question: What are the probabilities of getting something to happen if we send our members one by one unlinked to each other, as individual complainants or supplicants, as compared to sending one or two of them (or more) as representatives of a group formed with an interest in this problem? What are the probabilities of getting something done if we send individuals one by one, followed by a presentation by a formal group concerned with this problem (or vice versa)?
   b. What effects do different kinds of groups have on getting change? Participants may want to consider experimentally (or in terms of "What if?") the following kinds of questions: If a group presentation is used, what should be the nature of that group? Should we present ourselves as persons who are interested in "X," as students or as faculty interested in "X" (using our status), as a formal organization of persons formed to alter "X," etc.? If the last, what effects will the name of our organization have? Will we want to include an ethnic or minority interest in the problem? Will we want to be viewed as having a local base or a national base (real or potential)? Will we want to be viewed as an autonomous organization or as a subtask-force of a national (or regional) organization? Will we want to be viewed as a philanthropic, educational, political, or religious body? Will we want to be seen as against something or for something? How will these decisions affect our likelihood of access and effecting change?

3. Having made decisions concerning individual-group strategies, how do you decide what form of communication will be effective?
   a. What effects do different forms of communication have on effecting change? The participants may want to experiment with (or imagine with the "What if?" question) how contact should be made. For example, what are the consequences of using the telephone to register a complaint or make a request as compared to a face-to-face interview, as compared to a formal letter (with or without a formal letterhead)? What effects do face-to-face interviews have when they are not followed up as compared to

follow-up with confirming letters, phone calls, telegrams, etc.? How does the ordering of the forms of communication affect the outcome (persistence-resistance-persistence)? Participants may also want to look at how they divide the labor among themselves and how (and if) task specialists develop.

b. Who should make the contact? What effect does one person representing a group have in contrast to two, four, twenty, etc., in a face-to-face interaction? That is, if face-to-face interaction is chosen, what is the optimal number of group representatives?

c. How should the persons in face-to-face interaction present themselves in terms of status cues? What kind of presentation of self is likely to effect the change? Will standard American presentations of high status or low status work? Will presentations of other lifestyles (subcultures) be more effective? Participants may want to experiment with all having the same request (a request that can only be granted to an individual as an individual, such as library privileges) to discover what kinds of persons (in terms of status cues) are more likely to be granted the request.

d. How should participants present themselves in terms of other nonverbal dimensions? How can they use kinesics, proxemics, chronemics, and paralinguistics to achieve their ends? They may wish to experiment with different tactics along these lines, for example, standing around an office waiting rather than making an appointment, or signalling friendliness and courtesy versus signalling anger and belligerence.

4. Having located the person or office responsible for the area in question, what routes to that access should be followed? (This overlaps with #2 and #3; that is, the decisions are interlinked.)

a. What route to access achieves what results? What happens if you go directly to the top as compared to up the chain of command? What happens if you go above the person or the office in question (bypassing that office entirely)? Will you be sent back down, or will the person above do your work for you? What happens if you use other relevant persons within the system, for example, if you go through the ombudsperson or the affirmative-action officer or the campus police? That is, what happens if you use the units already existing within the organization to enforce procedures or to handle complaints? What happens if you go to the press? What happens if you employ an informal network, using the influence of persons who are within the organization, but outside the area of complaint?

5. Assuming you have a problem you want changed, do you want to go it alone, as a group, or to increase your power base by drawing on other individuals and/or groups outside your task group?

a. If you choose the latter, what effects will that have on your group? Will new specialists (like external public-relations persons) develop? Will the solidarity of the group increase or decrease? Will the group have problems assimilating new members, coordinating with other groups, etc.? Will the rewards (the probability of achieving your ends) outweigh the costs (time, energy, coordination problems, etc.)? Will the group keep its eye on the goal or become immersed in the contract functions?

b. If you choose to increase your power base, how will you locate other groups or individuals? Petitions? The press? Placards? Bulletins? Letters to the editor? What appeals will work? Direct interaction with existing groups on campus (like the women's caucus, the black caucus, etc.)?

c. What effects will affiliation with other groups have on getting the change effected? That is, will you be judged by your "associations"? Will other organizations attempt to co-opt you?

d. Will you want to really increase your numbers or simply provide the illusion of large numbers? How would you go about that? Do the items under *b* above function in that way?

6. What tactics and strategies might be employed that completely circumvent the existing system? That is, can you achieve your goals more quickly and readily by going outside the system than by working within it? (It is presumed that participants will not use any methods that are illegal, unethical, or immoral.) What persons, organizations, institutions, outside the system will have what kinds of effect? Will a call to a senator do it? Will a call to a cleric do it? Will a public demonstration or picketing be effective? Will a "march" work? Will an article in the town paper work?

Exercise 10. Learning About Strategies for Change in Organizations

PURPOSE. The purpose of this exercise is to provide an alternative to the preceding section in terms of the organizational setting. That is, the same general purpose previously discussed (to learn about strategies and tactics for change through experimentation and discovery) is uppermost; but in this case, participants will be asked to leave the instructional setting and focus on an organization other than an educational one.

PROCEDURES. The procedures (in terms of the questions, strategies, and tactics) are the same as in the preceding section. However, participants should decide on a problem relevant to an organization outside the learning community. Some examples are the following:

1. The task group desires to have credit cards at the major department store in town.
2. The task group is concerned with the rights of welfare recipients and wants to gain information from the welfare agency (or agencies) about welfare rights.

3. The task group is interested in helping a particular welfare recipient who feels he or she is getting the runaround.
4. The task group wants to receive food stamps for a few weeks.
5. The task group wants to get a group library card which can be used at all libraries in town.
6. The task group (as a group) wants to get a bank loan to cover some short-term expenses.
7. The task group wants to find out about the "quality of life" in the town (infant mortality rates, crime rates, pollution, water purity, home ownership, etc.).
8. The task group wants to find a placement for a multihandicapped child (what services are available and how to get them).
9. The task group wants to incorporate as a tax-exempt nonprofit organization.
10. The task group wants to change the confusing highway markers on the freeway.

The task selected by the group may be as simple as finding out who is in charge of a certain area and managing to get access to that person (for example, talking to a bank president, store president, or Chamber of Commerce director), or it may be a more complicated civil task (like finding out information about the city other than what the Chamber of Commerce says, or altering some city-level procedure).

Exercise 11. Ethnomethodological Interventions in Restaurants (by Donald Cruickshank)

1. Order something that is not on the menu and insist that it be served to you because you have a special dietary problem.
2. Ask for a larger (or smaller) portion of food when it is served. Use retorts such as "This isn't enough to satisfy me" (or "This is too much and I don't want to waste food"). Don't eat unless there is a favorable response.
3. Ask that a table be moved to a more attractive place (for example, near a window) so that you can enjoy your meal more.
4. Ask that one side dish be substituted for another (for example, a vegetable).
5. Ask to see the kitchen to determine if it is clean before you eat there. Ask for evidence that the restaurant is licensed by the Board of Health.
6. Change your mind after you are served, but before you begin to eat. Ask for something your companion ordered because "it looks better."
7. Ask to be served by another waitress who is at a different station. Decline to move—ask that the waitress move.
8. Ask for a salad dressing that is not available. Suggest that it would be simple enough to get some from the nearby grocery.

8. Try to pay half of your bill with cash or a check and put the rest on your credit card.
10. Ask for a chair that fits your size more comfortably—either larger or smaller.

SUGGESTED READINGS

Ethnomethodology

Berger, P. *The social construction of reality.* Garden City, N.Y.: Anchor-Doubleday, 1967.
Cicourel, A. *The social organization of juvenile justice.* New York: Wiley, 1968.
Cicourel, A. Ethnomethodology. In *Cognitive sociology.* New York: Free Press, 1974.
Douglas, J., ed. *Understanding everyday life.* Chicago: Aldine, 1970.
Goffman, E. *Asylums: Essays on the social situation of mental patients and other inmates.* Garden City, N.Y.: Anchor-Doubleday, 1961.
Goffman, E. *Behavior in public places.* Glencoe, Ill.: Free Press, 1963.
Goffman, E. *Interaction ritual.* Garden City, N.Y.: Anchor-Doubleday, 1967.
Hill, R., & Crittendon, K., eds. *Proceedings of the Purdue Symposium on Ethnomethodology.* Lafayette, Ind.: Purdue University, Institute for the Study of Social Change and Department of Sociology, 1968.
Mehan, H., & Wood, H. *The reality of ethnomethodology.* New York: Wiley-Interscience, 1975.
Mullins, N. Ethnomethodology. The speciality that came in from the cold. In *Theories and theory groups in contemporary American sociology.* New York: Harper & Row, 1973. Pp. 181-205.
Sudnow, D., ed. *Studies in social interaction.* New York: Free Press, 1972.
Turner, R. ed. *Ethnomethodology.* Middlesex, England: Penguin Publishers, 1974.

Communications

Birdwhistell, R.L. *Kinesics and context: Essays on body motion.* Philadelphia: University of Pennsylvania Press, 1970.
Bruyn, S. Appendix B: Phenomenological procedures. In *The human perspective in sociology.* Englewood Cliffs, N.Y.: Prentice-Hall, 1966. Pp. 271-281.
Folb, E. A. *A comparative study of urban black argot.* Occasional Papers in Linguistics, No. 1. Los Angeles: University of California at Los Angeles, 1972.
Hall, E. T. *The silent language.* Greenwich, Conn.: Fawcett Publishing, 1959.
Hall, E. T. *The hidden dimension.* Garden City, N.Y.: Anchor-Doubleday, 1966.
Kochman, T., ed. *Rappin' and stylin' out: Communication in urban black America.* Urbana: University of Illinois Press, 1972.
Nehrabian, A. *Nonverbal communication.* Chicago: Aldine, 1972.
Scheflen, A. E. *Body language and the social order.* Englewood Cliffs, N.J.: Prentice-Hall, 1972.
Scheflen, A. E. *How behavior means.* Garden City, N.Y.: Anchor-Doubleday, 1974.
Speier, M. *How to observe face-to-face communication.* Pacific Palisades, Calif.: Goodyear Publishing Co., 1973.
Sommer, R. *Personal space: The behavioral basis of design.* Englewood Cliffs, N.J.: Prentice-Hall, 1969.
Weitz, S. *Nonverbal communication: Readings with commentary.* New York: Oxford University Press, 1974.

Postscript

A famous sociologist, Max Weber, once pondered the beginnings of what has come to be known as "The Organizational Revolution" and became concerned that the western world is becoming too rational. He feared that much of the magic and the mystery that throughout history has enriched life with a sense of enchantment would disappear.

Perhaps Weber was correct about the loss of enchantment, but we still find plenty of *mystery* in life, and organizations seem to be responsible for much of it. Despite the emergence of a so-called "Science of Organizational Behavior" during the past generation or so, there is still much to be learned about organizations. However, some progress has also been made as, indeed, we hope this series of volumes has demonstrated.

Perhaps it would be instructive to pause at this point to review some of the contributions that have been made to date. For reasons to be explained later, we suggest that there is probably no better place to start than with the popular literature that has been published on this subject in recent decades.

Some obscure person with no first name, referred to as Murphy, is said to have formulated the first law on organizations. "Murphy's Law" is:

- If anything *can* go wrong it *will*.

In fact, Murphy seems to have formulated a law for every occasion. Among them are these:

- Nothing is ever as simple as it first seems.
- Everything you decide to do costs more than first estimated.
- Every activity takes more time than you have.
- Whatever you set out to do, something else must be done first.
- If you improve or tinker with something long enough, eventually it will break.
- By making something absolutely clear, somebody will be confused.
- You can fool some of the people all of the time and all of the people some of the time—and that is sufficient.

These principles have provided a solid foundation upon which many other scholars have been able to build. Consider these provocative disclosures:

- Weller's Law: "Nothing is impossible for the man who doesn't have to do it himself." (1)

- Chisholm's Second Law of Human Interaction: "Any time things appear to be going better, you have overlooked something." (2)
- Shanahan's Law: "The length of a meeting rises with the square of the number of people present." (3)
- Finagle's Law: "Once a job is fouled up, anything done to improve it makes it worse." (4)
- Rudin's Law: "In a crisis that forces a choice to be made among alternative courses of action, most people will choose the worst one possible." (5)
- Crane's Law: "There is no such thing as a free lunch." (6)

Notwithstanding these impressive contributions, there has been some disagreement about the relative importance of Murphy. At least some scholars assign greater stature to a writer who does have a first name, C. Northcote Parkinson. It is of course he who formulated the well-known law that he modestly dubbed, "Parkinson's Law," to wit:

- Work expands to fill the time available. (*Parkinson's Law,* Houghton and Mifflin, 1960.)

From this simple proposition he derived several corollaries, including these gems:

- Expenditure rises to meet income (Parkinson's second law).
- Time spent on any item of an (meeting) agenda will be in inverse proportion to the sum of money involved.
- There is an inverse relationship between the opulence of the office decor of a firm and its solvency.

In addition to these shattering principles, Parkinson discovered the formulae for (a) determining the number of committee members necessary to make the working of a committee manifestly impossible, and (b) pinpointing the exact location of the most important people at a cocktail party, based on the leftward and centrifugal flow of human movement.

Another breakthrough was made recently by Lawrence J. Peter. According to his "Peter Principle:"

- In a hierarchy, every employee tends to rise to his/her level of incompetence.

That is, once a person has become competent in a particular job, he/she is promoted to a new job for which that person has no demonstrated competence. Unfortunately we cannot think of examples.

To these fundamental laws we would modestly add our own:

- There is always opposition to everything.

Paralleling these theoretical developments, and partly stimulated by them, there is a body of more applied work intended to help individuals cope with their own organizations, such as Townsand's popular, *Up The*

Organization. Stephen Potter's *One Upsmanship* (Holt, 1952) is another example. This obscure classic advises people on how to manage every conceivable social situation they might encounter, from how to impress people when entering an art gallery (ploys and gambits connected with the art of being, or seeming to be, a visitor to an art exhibition) to basic clubmanship and doctorship (advice based on the natural one-downness of the patient). Potter is at his best when advising college students that the under-graduate-man must give one of two impressions, either that he does nothing but work, or that he does no work. To impress student watchers, Potter advises striding into the reading room with hat on, going directly to the shelves of a subject one is not necessarily studying, taking out a book as if one knew where to look for it, running down a reference, and walking out again "quietly but plonkingly."

The field of hierarchiology reached a new plateau with the 1977 publication of Harold Morowitz's *Ego Niches* (Ox Bow Press). The author, a biologist, has for the first time discovered and catalogued many of the human species that inhabit various niches within organizations. The theory is based on these obviously valid postulates:

- The primary functions of any organization are performed by people in the lower echelons;
- The higher one climbs in the hierarchy, the more time one must spend justifying what one is doing;
- The higher one looks in a hierarchy, the more likely one is to find incompetent people doing unnecessary work totally unrelated to the primary purpose of the organization. (This postulate represents a convergence with the "Peter Principle.")

With this disarmingly simple theory, the author has already discovered several species. Only a few can be mentioned here:

1. *The Octopus niche:* this small office holds the specialist surrounded by technical books and desk calculators, who fends off predators by spewing out large quantities of murky ink in the form of memos, printouts, reports, copies, charts, graphs, and the like.
2. *The Howler Monkey niche:* inhabited by packs of people who guard their territorial domains with busy work and verbal attacks on interlopers (complaints and gossip).
3. *The Beaver niche:* occupied by insecure individuals who are so anxious to please the boss that they overwhelm everyone with work; they find so many options and produce so many informative memos that things get dammed up for everybody else.
4. *The Puffer Fish niche:* here the self-important person who is too small for the job, creatively guards his ego with ritualistic displays of clothing and uniforms, name dropping, and especially by remaining always inaccessible.
5. *The Giraffe niche:* a tall and narrow place for the enviable person with his head in the clouds who is able to remain serenely aloof from everything that happens about him.

6. *The Sand Crab niche:* for the career person who defends his position by giving the appearance of being constantly busy at his job while forever moving sideways.

Perhaps the reader is wondering why we have chosen to dwell upon these popular works when there is voluminous literature of serious scholarship on organizations that deserves mention. Our choice has been deliberate. For the popular literature is a formal expression of what can be termed "street knowledge," the informal theories of organization that each of us has fashioned from our own experiences with organizations. The very popularity of these works demonstrates beyond doubt that each of us needs and uses organizational theories. We could not get along without them. And moreover, we believe that theory derived from such street knowledge should be seriously considered by social scientists.

The fact is that experience-based theory is often so convincing that by comparison it is tempting to depreciate so-called "scientific" theory. Many persons are probably inclined to agree with C. Northcote Parkinson (p. vii) when he states that:

> Heaven forbid that students should cease to read books on the science of public or business administration—provided only that these works are classified as fiction. Placed between the novels of Rider Haggard and H. G. Wells, intermingled with volumes about ape men and space ships, these textbooks could harm no one.

And, it is easy to be skeptical about social science. For example, consider the so-called "Law of Propinquity," namely that marriages tend to occur among people who reside near one another; or conversely, people in this country who have not met seldom marry. Such propositions hardly seem more advanced than conventional wisdom. In fact, hasn't everyone always known that "birds of a feather flock together"?

However, there is also a problem with conventional wisdom. It tells us something else: "opposites attract." If birds of a feather flock together, then how can opposites attract? When the question is posed in this way, one can begin to see the role of social science in relation to conventional wisdom. In addition to discovering new principles, and this too often fails to occur, social science can help identify and unravel the *conditions* when propositions in the store of conventional wisdom apply and when they do not.

One has only to consider the movie (and the book) *Up the Down Staircase,* a portrait of New York City teachers that was discussed in Volume II of this series. It exemplifies many popular works characterizing teachers as docile, compliant employees dominated by administrators and overwhelmed by the bureaucracy. And yet, it must be remembered that the play-it-safe teachers that Bel Kaufman describes, during the 1960's were involved in some of the most rancorous teacher strikes in the history of American education. It is not meaningful to ask whether these teachers are "really" as compliant as Kaufman portrays them or as rebellious as they are painted in the news media. The question is, under what conditions have various groups of teachers in New York City and elsewhere acted aggressively and when have they been more docile, and why? This is one place social science can make a contribution.

The authors of the literature we have cited are of course writing largely with tongue-in-cheek. But, they are also sounding warnings about a serious issue: the capacity of organizations to overwhelm individuals and thus eventually overpower and distort their social purposes. Is it true that members of organizations eventually lose sight of organizational purposes and is it true that they are rewarded for adapting to organizations as they presently exist? Can well-meaning individuals be molded into creatures of organizations? And if it is possible, is it inevitable?

Large organizations are essential for industrialized society, and indeed for modern democracy. However, their powers can seriously impair the ability of employees of service organizations to serve their publics. A challenge, then, is to find ways to curb the power of organizations without destroying their advantages. We believe that by reflecting upon organizations, people can learn how to resist some of the worst features of organizations and how to unleash the positive potential that is inherent in modern organizations.

In short, social scientists can, and often must start with the same street knowledge that most citizens use everyday. It is then their job to test and refine this knowledge in order to make it more useful. Social science and conventional wisdom feed upon one another; hence, social scientists, practitioners and other laymen must collaborate to build a valid and useful body of organizational theory.

It is on this premise that we have launched this series of volumes. We hope that the series will prompt you, our readers, to go well beyond this brief introduction to the study of organizations. And we hope that you—whether practitioners or social scientists—will try, as we have tried, to cross the boundary of social science and practice with collaborators whose colleagueship might prove as valuable and intellectually stimulating as ours has been.

FOOTNOTES

[1] A. H. Weiler, movie editor of *The New York Times,* in a privately circulated memorandum.
[2] Quoted by Rovert M. Porter, Professor of Education, State University, Onconta, N.Y. in the *Saturday Review,* Feb. 1, 1964: Chisholm unidentified.
[3] Eileen Shanahan, economics reporter for *The New York Times.*
[4] Quoted by Brooks Atkinson in *The New York Times,* Feb. 1, 1963; Finagle unidentified.
[5] S. A. Rudin of Atlanta in a letter to the *New Republic,* 1961.
[6] Burton Crane, *The Sophisticated Investor* (Simon and Schuster, 1959).

Appendix
Instructional Mode, Goals, and Objectives*

INSTRUCTIONAL MODE

The instructional mode used during the Corps Member Training Institute was important in ensuring the effectiveness of the materials and the favorable responses of participants. Suggestions for the mode and tone of instruction follow:

1. *Instruction should occur in small groups.* Ideally participants should be organized in basic discussion groups of about 10 members with one instructor for each group. Diversity of background among group members with one instructor is highly desirable. Instructors should be flexible and vary the program to meet the demands of an evolving instructional process.
2. *Instruction should give attention to the needs and interests of participants.* The backgrounds and levels of sophistication of participants should be assessed prior to, or at the first meeting, so that planning and grouping is responsive to the diversity and needs of participants.
3. *Instructional expectations should be made public.* Participants should receive statements of training goals and objectives, how those goals and objectives will be achieved, and indicators of how the participants will be evaluated.
4. *Instruction should provide for intensive involvement of participants.* Special effort should be made to select case studies, papers, vignettes, readings, abstracts, and films that are particularly suited to participants who are preservice or inservice teachers. Small group discussion should be planned to give every participant an active part in establishing a rationale, making choices and decisions, and testing principles and theories inherent in different kinds of organizations.
5. *Instruction should capitalize on the temporary society created by the group itself.* Characteristics of the group, as illustrated in its governance and its social and work problems, may be used for analysis and diagnosis, providing a real situation with which individuals and groups can deal.
6. *Instruction should deal with process problems and skills as part of instruction.* How and why people behave in certain ways in an

---

*Reprinted from Volume I of this series by Corwin and Edelfelt, Perspectives on Organizations: Viewpoints for Teachers (Washington, D.C.: American Association of Colleges for Teacher Education, 1976), pp. 8-10.

organization is part of learning about organizations. As appropriate, participants should use illustrations of their own behavior to analyze why particular progress or achievement by a group has or has not been made.

7. *Instruction should engage participants directly with problems of analysis, diagnosis, and choice.* In part, this point reiterates numbers 4 and 5. In addition, participants should have instructors and speakers interpret and discuss field experiences, role-playing situations, and other experiences. In all of these activities, the purpose is to deal directly and personally with how effectively one can work through a problem in a logical, rational way.

8. *Instruction should provide a variety of activities.* Engaging the interest of people in studying organizations is not easy. A variety of activities enriches the training session; for example, case studies, film and vignette analysis, field-based study of various organizations, independent study, readings, and films which are appropriate for use in groups of various sizes.

9. *Instruction should include close guidance, monitoring, and evaluation of participants.* The instructor-participant ratio should allow some one-to-one contact, providing opportunities to discuss how the goals of the program fit those of the individual and to negotiate modifications when possible. Such modifications, of course, become a matter of record and provide some data for program evaluation. The instructor's responsibility for evaluation is continuous and should be done cooperatively with participants.

10. *Instruction should respect the status of all participants.* Although all participants (and instructors as well) are learners, each participant presumably has a different status based on his or her competence, experience, and power position. This is especially true if a group contains both preservice and inservice teachers. Each person's place in the hierarchy should be recognized and respected.

We recognize that these 10 points are appropriate to study in any field and all too often are unattainable for one or more reasons. Yet, a large part of the success of the Corps Member Training Institute was attributable to a continuous effort to follow these principles. Each person using this material for instructional purposes will need to decide how best to present the concepts based on ever-changing tradeoffs among instructors' skills, learners' needs, and administrative support systems.

GOALS AND OBJECTIVES

The materials contained in Parts I and II of this book work together, enabling participants to achieve certain goals and objectives. The goals and objectives are shared with participants so that everyone is aware of the purposes for studying organizations.

The overall goal of *Perspectives on Organizations* is to:
- Develop an awareness of the characteristics and functions of organizations, and of how organizations and individuals influence each other.

The program designed to help participants reach this goal includes instruction to:
- Enable participants to identify problems that result from or are aggravated by some characteristics of organizations.
- Provide participants with skills, enabling them to analyze organizations and organizational problems.
- Build participant interest in continuing independent study of organizations in the future.

When they have completed the program, participants should be able to demonstrate (through analysis and discussion of organizations) that they have:
- An understanding of why it is important to study organizations.
- A knowledge of some of the complexities resulting from membership in organizations.
- The ability to define organizations, social systems, bureaucracy, organization theory.
- An awareness of approaches used to study organizations.
- An awareness of some key features of organizations.
- An understanding of how the various functions of organizations are coordinated.
- An awareness of models that are useful for analyzing organizations.
- The ability to classify organizations according to typology.
- An understanding of how the social environment might affect the organization.
- A knowledge of strategies for coping in organizations.

These, and perhaps other objectives that participants will identify for themselves, should be achieved as a study proceeds. Participants and instructors will frequently want to refer back to these objectives to assess progress. The materials and activities designed to help achieve the objectives are contained in each book in this series.

207065-C.2